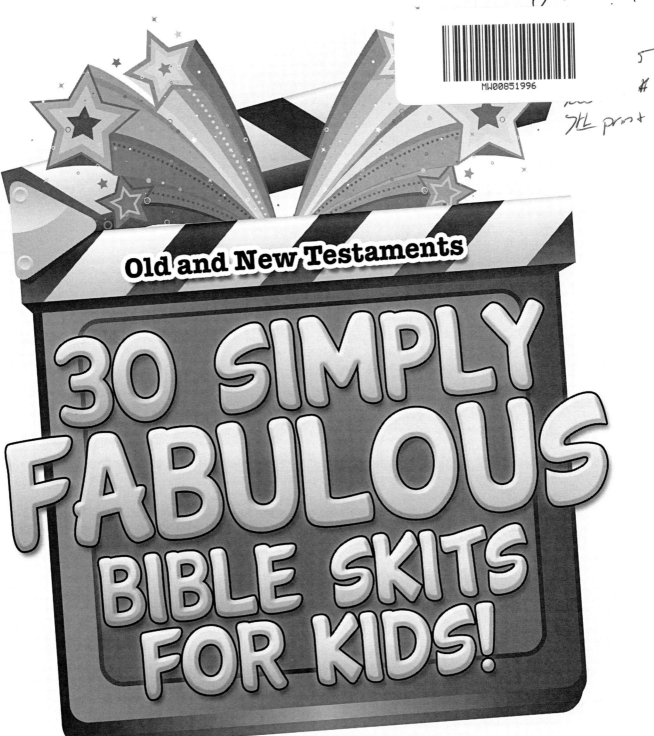

Old and New Testaments

30 SIMPLY FABULOUS BIBLE SKITS FOR KIDS!

by Steven James

DEDICATION
To Robin,
for believing in these stories
and that they need to be retold.

Warner Press, Inc
Warner Press and "WP" logo are trademarks of Warner Press, Inc

30 Simply Fabulous Bible Skits for Kids
by Steven James

Requests for information should be sent to:
Warner Press, Inc
1201 East Fifth Street
P.O. Box 2499
Anderson, IN 46012
www.warnerpress.org

Editor: Robin Fogle
Designer: Curtis D. Corzine

ISBN: 978-1-59317-793-5

Printed in USA

TABLE OF CONTENTS

How to Use This Book

These skits (otherwise known as reader's theatre scripts) are super-easy to use and aren't intimidating for students because there aren't any lines to memorize.

Just choose your story, photocopy the scripts, hand them out to your students, and you have an instant lesson.

Each kid-friendly skit retells a Bible story in a fun and creative way using 3-12 students. The stories are written for live presentation. They can be performed using actors and actresses, puppets, or a mixture of the two. You could even record students reading the parts for an old-fashioned radio show.

Here are some simple steps to take to make the most of this book:

STEP #1 – READ THE SCRIPT.
Before class, read through the complete skit and look for any words or concepts that your students might not understand. Pay special attention to unusual names that your students might not recognize or be able to pronounce. Later, when you call the children forward to present the story, you can tell them how to pronounce the unusual names.

You may wish to glance through the Table of Contents and the Scripture Verse Index to find just the right story for your group.

STEP #2 – ASSIGN PARTS.
As you review the script, consider which of your students would best fit the different reading parts. Typically, the narrator of the story has the longest reading parts and should be more experienced at reading aloud. For all the parts, you'll want to choose children who are comfortable reading aloud and presenting in front of a group. Some parts are humorous and contain silly comments or jokes. Don't be afraid to choose kids who like to ham it up for those parts!

If you have younger children in your class or children who aren't comfortable reading in front of others, you could use adults or teen volunteers to read the scripts instead. The reading level is targeted for 3rd-4th grade and up.

STEP #3 – RESEARCH THE STORY.
Look up the story in the Bible. Scripture references are included with each skit. Read the story to understand its context. The skits are based on Bible stories but have been adapted for live performance. Some stories are condensed or revised, and others include only selective parts of the story so that it remains age-appropriate for children.

You'll want to familiarize yourself with the Bible story so you can answer any questions that might arise after the skit has been presented.

STEP #4 – PHOTOCOPY THE SCRIPTS.
If you have enough copies of this book to give one to each child, do that. Otherwise, you'll need to photocopy enough copies of the scripts to give one copy to each of the readers. (Photocopy permission is granted for this purpose.) Make one extra copy for yourself so you can follow along and help prompt a child if she can't find her part, or stumbles over the pronunciation of a word. You may wish to place each script in a black folder (or a different colored folder for each part) so the audience doesn't see the scripts. It's a little touch, but it can add class to the performance.

Use a highlight marker to identify the speaking parts for each specific story character. This makes it much easier for children to locate their lines and follow along in their script.

Decide whether or not you wish to use any costumes or props for the story. If there are suggested props for the story, gather those at this time.

STEP #5 – HAND OUT THE SCRIPTS.

Now that you've familiarized yourself with the story, identified any sections that might cause your students to stumble, and chosen which students to call forward, your before-class preparation is done. Your next step is to bring the students up and hand out the scripts.

Give them a moment to look over the scripts while you introduce the story. (Note: Depending on the confidence you have in the reading ability of your students, you may wish to give them the scripts before class and let them practice before performing the story in front of the group. Also, make sure your readers know that they're not supposed to read the italicized stage directions aloud.)

In most cases, it's not crucial whether you choose a boy or a girl for a specific reading part. Sometimes it might be funny to have a girl play a part that is obviously a boy's part (such as Samson), or a boy play a girl's part (such as Delilah). In any case, if you reverse gender roles be sure you mention that to the audience. Children won't always know just by the names if a Bible character is male or female, and you don't want them to be confused or misinformed.

Use discretion about whether or not to choose girls for reading parts that involve Jesus or God the Father. There are specific theological reasons why Jesus was male (for example, He is the Groom and gave up His life for His bride, the Church—see Ephesians 5:25, Mark 2:19-20. And God was Jesus' Father, not His mother—Mary was).

STEP #6 – SIT BACK AND ENJOY!

Once you're ready to begin, go and sit toward the front of the class with the rest of the listeners. Say, "OK, let's give them a hand and get started! Lights...Camera...Action!"

Don't stay onstage with the students while they're performing because they'll naturally look to you for prompts and help if they get lost. If a director stands onstage, children often turn their backs to the audience and face the director instead. Also, you can coach and direct your

actors and actresses more easily from the front row of the audience.

When the skit is finished, lead the listeners in applauding for the readers to thank them for their hard work!

WHAT DO I NEED TO TELL THE STUDENTS ABOUT ACTING AND PERFORMING?

Encourage the students to look up at the audience whenever possible during the story so their eyes aren't on the scripts the whole time. At first they might not look up at all, but their eye contact will improve the more they practice performing skits and the more comfortable they become reading aloud.

Tell them, "Remember not to hold the script in front of your face. The audience will want to see you while you're reading! And never turn your back to the listeners. Remember, you're telling the story to them, not to the other people on stage."

Remind the students not to go on with their lines if the audience is busy laughing. Wait until the laughter dies down before continuing, or no one will hear the words.

Sometimes one student might be a little slow in finding his or her lines. When that happens, the other readers might say something like, "Hey! Narrator! Say your part!" Stop this if you see it happening. Instead, encourage your students not to interrupt or correct each other, but only to read their own lines and leave the prompting to you, the director.

As the children perform, you may wish to encourage them to act out certain parts of the story. For example, when Goliath gets killed you could say, "OK, Goliath, fall over dead!" For the most part though, encourage them only to act out those things specifically mentioned in the scripts. Otherwise, they might get confused or lose their place.

CAN I CHANGE THE SCRIPTS IN THIS BOOK?

Feel free to make minor editorial changes to the scripts in this book. You may wish to leave out a joke that wouldn't make sense to your listeners or delete a phrase that might be misunderstood. However, permission is not granted to alter the stories in such a way that you change the theological meaning or intent of the story.

DO WE NEED SPECIAL COSTUMES OR PROPS?

Unless otherwise noted, no special costumes are needed for the stories. However, you may wish to use some silly costumes for various characters or stories. Use general stage lighting and microphones if your audience is large. Make sure the listeners can hear the performers and won't be distracted by other things going on in the room.

WHY DO WE STILL TELL BIBLE STORIES TODAY?

Psalm 78:1-7 (NLT) explains that we share God's ancient stories so this generation, and the ones to come, will turn to the Lord and place their faith in Him:

O my people, listen to my instructions.
Open your ears to what I am saying,
for I will speak to you in a parable.
I will teach you hidden lessons from our past—
stories we have heard and known,
stories our ancestors handed down to us.
We will not hide these truths from our children;
we will tell the next generation
about the glorious deeds of the LORD,
about his power and his mighty wonders.
For he issued his laws to Jacob;
he gave his instructions to Israel.
He commanded our ancestors
to teach them to their children,
so the next generation might know them—
even the children not yet born—
and they in turn will teach their own children.
So each generation should set its hope anew on God,
not forgetting his glorious miracles
and obeying his commands.

In addition, the stories of the Bible were written to teach us and give us hope: *For everything that was written in the past was written to teach us, so that through the endurance taught in the Scriptures and the encouragement they provide we might have hope* (Romans 15:4, NIV).

Finally, stories of people's struggles in the Bible serve as examples of moral choices and warnings about the consequences of sin. Why? *To keep us from setting our hearts on evil things as they did.... These things happened to them as examples and were written down as warnings for us (*1 Corinthians 10:6, 11, NIV).

So use these stories for instruction, encouragement, and warning.

SUMMARY

As you present these stories, remember to encourage your students to face the audience and use plenty of facial expressions, sound effects, and natural gestures. Encourage them to respond to the audience, have fun, and enjoy themselves!

ADAM, EVE, AND A SNEAKY SNAKE

BASED ON: Genesis 2–3

BIG IDEA: God created Adam and Eve and gave them a beautiful garden to live in. God commanded Adam and Eve not to eat fruit from a certain tree in the garden. When they disobeyed Him, He showed mercy and love by promising them a Savior (see Genesis 3:15).

BACKGROUND: God spoke the world into existence and called everything He had made "good." After Adam realized there was no companion for him, he felt lonely. The first thing that God ever said wasn't good about His creation was Adam's loneliness. God then created Eve from Adam's rib. At last God finished His creation. He told Adam, "You are free" (see Genesis 2:15). But Adam and Eve didn't honor God in their freedom. When Satan, in the form of a snake, tempted Eve, she gave in. Pretty soon, Adam had joined her in her sin. When God confronted them, they discovered they would have to leave God's garden, but He still had mercy for them.

NEW TESTAMENT CONNECTION: God created us to live in community with each other. We're designed to both need and help each other. Believers are told to love each other (1 Peter 1:22, 1 John 4:11, Romans 13:8), accept one another (Romans 15:7), serve one another (Galatians 5:13), be kind to one another (Ephesians 4:32), forgive one another (Galatians 3:13), and encourage one another (Hebrews 3:13).

In Romans 5, Paul explains that since sin entered the world through one man (Adam), sin can be forgiven by one man (Jesus Christ). Sometimes in the New Testament Jesus is referred to as the "New Adam" since He was tempted yet never gave in to sin.

CAST: You'll need 5-6 children for this skit: Narrator (girl or boy), Eve (preferably a girl), Adam (preferably a boy), God (boy), Serpent (girl or boy), Tree (adult, optional)

PROPS: A piece of fruit and a rubber snake (both optional)

TOPICS: Creation, family relationships, friendship, loneliness, new life, choices, consequences, death, following God, forgiveness, God's love, God's promises, grace, hiding, hope, listening to God, obedience, rebellion, second chances, sin, talking animals, temptation

TIPS: If you wish, you can invite a person up to be the Tree. Hand him a piece of fruit and tell him to make his arms into branches. If you choose a man or adult for this part, when the script describes the Serpent being in the Tree, encourage the Serpent to climb up onto the shoulders or on the back of the person playing the Tree. Have fun with this part!

Position the students onstage with the Serpent and the Narrator to the left, the Tree and Adam and Eve in the middle, and God on the far right.

Bring up the stage lights, and then begin when the listeners are quiet.

Adam, Eve, and a Sneaky Snake

DIRECTOR: Lights! Camera! Action!

NARRATOR: When God was creating the world, all types of fish and birds and animals appeared.

GOD: Let there be hippos! Let there be butterflies!

NARRATOR: Poof! There were hippos and butterflies!

GOD: Let there be a moon!

NARRATOR: Wham! There was the moon!

GOD: Let there be all kinds of cool stuff!

NARRATOR: Zowie! There was all kinds of cool stuff!

GOD: *(Smiling and nodding)* That's good....

NARRATOR: But God hadn't made any animals that could talk to Him or walk with Him, or understand right from wrong, or imagine or dream or believe in Him as their Savior.

GOD: Hmm... I'm not quite done yet. I'm gonna make someone special!

NARRATOR: So God came down to the earth and reached into the soil and formed a person.

GOD: I'll make a man out of mud.

ADAM: That's me—Mud Man!

NARRATOR: No, you're Adam.

ADAM: Hey, why didn't God call me "Clay"? That would have been appropriate.

NARRATOR: "Adam" means "from the land."

ADAM: I am Land Man! Do I get a trusty sidekick named Soil Boy?

NARRATOR: Adam didn't have a trusty sidekick—yet.

GOD: There! Now I'm almost done with my creation.

NARRATOR: Now God was no longer alone. He had Adam to stay with Him and play with Him and walk with Him and talk with Him…

ADAM: A human walkie-talkie!

NARRATOR: and God gave Adam the job of taking care of the beautiful new world.

GOD: Adam, take care of the beautiful new world.

ADAM: Okee-dokee, God.

NARRATOR: Then God let Adam name the animals. God sent them past, and Adam gave them names….

ADAM: Betsy...Fred...Gertrude...Ann...Julie... Bob...

NARRATOR: Um...not quite. Things like, "Hippo! Dodo bird!" Names like that.

ADAM: Oh. Hippo. Dodo bird. Dinosaur. Oranga...Orange mango...Orgotango... Um...Monkey...

NARRATOR: But as Adam watched the animals go past, he didn't see any that could stay with him and play with him and walk with him and talk with him.

ADAM: No more walkie-talkies. Hmm... These are all nice and everything, but I'd really like a sidekick.

NARRATOR: When God saw that Adam was lonely, for the first time ever, the Lord said that something in His world wasn't good.

GOD: It's not good for Adam to be lonely! I'm gonna make a partner and a friend for him.

ADAM: A sidekick!

GOD: Close enough.

NARRATOR: So God caused Adam to get very sleepy.

GOD: You are getting very sleepy...sleepy....

ADAM: Um, no I'm not, God. I'm not sleepy at all.

GOD: Yes, you are! I'm God, believe me... you're getting sleepy!

ADAM: *(Yawning)* Oh, right...sleepy.... I guess I could use a little nap. *(Snore! Snore!...)*

NARRATOR: Then God took one of Adam's ribs and formed a woman. When Adam woke up, there was a lady lying right next to him.

ADAM: Whoa! Who are you?

EVE: I'm Eve.

ADAM:	Can I call you Mrs. Sidekick?
EVE:	Um, no.
ADAM:	What about Mrs. Spare Rib?
EVE:	Not a chance.
ADAM:	Okay.
GOD:	Adam, this is your new wife, Eve!
ADAM:	Where's my old wife?
GOD:	You didn't have one.
ADAM:	Oh... Hi, Eve!
EVE:	Hi, Adam.
NARRATOR:	And so, Adam was no longer alone.
ADAM:	Cool.
NARRATOR:	Eve was no longer a rib.
EVE:	Cool.
NARRATOR:	And God had finally finished creating His wonderful world.
GOD:	*(Smiling and nodding)* Cool. And VERY good. I'd give it two thumbs up!
NARRATOR:	Then God put Adam and Eve in a beautiful garden. He gave them instructions on how to live there.
GOD:	You are free to eat of all the trees in the garden!
ADAM AND EVE:	*(Together)* Cool.
GOD:	But if you eat of the Tree of Knowledge of Good and Evil, you will die.
ADAM AND EVE:	*(Together)* Bummer.
NARRATOR:	So one day Adam and Eve were walking around and came near the tree that God had warned them about. Hanging from the tree was a snake.
SERPENT:	*(If you have a person playing the TREE, climb up onto his back or jump up into his arms. If desired, wave the rubber snake as you talk.)* Did God really say you couldn't eat any fruit in His garden?
EVE:	Of course, we can eat the fruit. But there's this one tree we can't eat from or touch. If we do, we'll die.

ADAM:	Bummer.
NARRATOR:	Now, Eve wasn't remembering exactly what God had said. She was changing it around. And so was the snake!
SERPENT:	You won't die! You'll get smarter! You'll be like God!
NARRATOR:	When Eve heard that, she took some fruit and ate it.
EVE:	Yummy!
NARRATOR:	Then she gave some to Adam.
ADAM:	Cool...and yummy!
NARRATOR:	But as soon as they'd eaten it, they knew they were going to die…
ADAM AND EVE:	*(Together)* Bummer.
NARRATOR:	because they weren't living God's way. Then God came looking for them.
GOD:	Hey! Where are you guys?
NARRATOR:	They hid from God because they were ashamed...and naked.
ADAM AND EVE:	*(Together)* Ah! Bummer. (*Cross your arms in front of you like you're covering your nakedness.*)
NARRATOR:	God told them they had messed up big time.
GOD:	You guys have messed up big time.
ADAM AND EVE:	*(Together)* We know.
GOD:	You're gonna have to leave the garden... and you're gonna die.
ADAM AND EVE:	*(Together)* Bummer.
NARRATOR:	But God promised them a Savior.
ADAM AND EVE::	*(Together)* Cool.
NARRATOR:	That Savior would be their only hope to be close to God again. And ever since then, believing in Him has been the only hope for us, too.
EVERYONE:	*(Together)* The end!

(Smile, bow, and then take your seat.)

NOAH AND THE ZOO CRUISE

BASED ON: Genesis 6–9

BIG IDEA: God kept His promise to rescue Noah and his family from the worldwide flood. God keeps His promises to us today too.

BACKGROUND: After God created the world, the people soon turned away from Him. The rebellion on the earth became so bad that God decided to destroy His new world with a cataclysmic flood. However, Noah and his family trusted and followed God.

God told Noah to build an ark. Then God sent him two of each of the different types of animals in the world so that he could rescue them.

NEW TESTAMENT CONNECTION: Because of his faith in God, Noah was recognized by God as righteous (see Hebrews 11:7). God is grieved by sin and judges it but is also gracious to those who love Him.

Also, in his letter to the early Christian church, Peter explains that the water of the flood symbolizes God's saving power through baptism (1 Peter 3:18-21).

CAST: You'll need 5 children for this skit: Narrator (girl or boy), Sound Effects Person (girl or boy), Noah's Wife (preferably a girl), Noah (preferably a boy), God (boy)

PROPS: A brown paper lunch bag (or an airplane barf bag); a bottle of bubbles and a bubble blower, or a spray bottle (all optional)

TOPICS: Anger, creation, faith, faithfulness, following God, God's power, God's promises, listening to God, obedience, second chances, sin

TIPS: You may wish to let the Sound Effects Person practice his lines before performing the drama. If you have a sound system, you may also want to give him a microphone. Sound effects always sound better through a microphone! Give the lunch bag to the Sound Effects Person (he or she will hand it to Noah's Wife when she starts to get seasick). And give him the bottle of bubbles (or spray bottle) too.

Position the Narrator and Sound Effects Person on the left side of the stage, Noah and Noah's Wife in the center, and God on the right side of the stage. Bring up the stage lights, and then begin when the students are quiet.

NOAH AND THE ZOO CRUISE

DIRECTOR: Lights! Camera! Action!

NARRATOR: Long ago, the people of the earth were very mean.

SOUND EFFECTS: *(Growl...scream...do a mad scientist-type evil laugh.)*

NARRATOR: What are you doing?

SOUND EFFECTS: I'm the sound effects person! *(Make the sound of a creaky door. Then do another mad scientist-type evil laugh.)*

NARRATOR: *(Rolling your eyes)* Oh, great.

SOUND EFFECTS: This is gonna be fun. Hee, hee, hee, hee.

NARRATOR: People were so mean that God felt sorry He'd ever made them in the first place.

GOD: I'll wipe 'em out and start over!

SOUND EFFECTS: *(Make the sound of an explosion.)* Boom!

GOD: But I'll save Noah because he believes in Me and follows Me.

SOUND EFFECTS: *(Very dramatically)* Hallelujah!

GOD: Hey, Noah!

NOAH: Yeah, God?

GOD: Build Me a boat.

NOAH: Am I going on a cruise?

GOD: Well, sort of.

NOAH: Can I take my wife?

GOD: Yeah. Take your whole family.

NOAH'S WIFE: Oh, goody. I hope it's to the Bahamas!

GOD: Not quite. It's a zoo cruise.

NOAH'S WIFE: Sounds exotic.

GOD: Oh, it is, believe Me. Now go and get started.

NOAH: Alrighty then!

NARRATOR: So Noah and his family built the boat.

SOUND EFFECTS: Hammer, hammer. Saw, saw. Hammer, hammer. Saw...

NOAH'S WIFE: Noah, where should I put the sail?

NOAH: It's not that kind of boat.

NOAH'S WIFE: Oh. Too bad.

NARRATOR: Year after year, they worked.

SOUND EFFECTS: *(Act tired.)* Hammer, hammer. Saw, saw. Hammer, hammer. Saw...

NOAH'S WIFE: This is the biggest boat I've ever seen.

NOAH: It's the only boat you've ever seen.

NOAH'S WIFE: Oh. Too bad.

NARRATOR: Until finally it was done.

NOAH'S WIFE: Whew.

NOAH: No kidding.

SOUND EFFECTS: You're telling me.

NARRATOR: And then God sent the animals. And they came to him two—

NOAH: I know this one! By fours!

NARRATOR: What?

NOAH: Two by fours!

NARRATOR: The animals didn't come in two by fours!

NOAH: The termites did.

NARRATOR: Look, the animals came to him two by two. And Noah and his family packed lots of food because they would have to feed all those animals and themselves.

SOUND EFFECTS: Chomp, chomp. Nibble, nibble. Chomp, chomp. Burp.

NOAH'S WIFE: That's a lot of doggie chow.

NARRATOR: They lived with those animals on the ark for a whole year.

NOAH'S WIFE: That's a lot of doggie poop.

EVERYONE: *(Together)* Yuck! *(Hold your nose.)*

NARRATOR: Then the wind and the rain started.

Sound Effects:	Whoosh! Whoosh! Spray, spray. Whoosh! Whoosh! Splash! *(Pull out the bottle of bubbles and blow them in the face of the NARRATOR or go nuts with the spray bottle.)*
Narrator:	Noah and his family and all those animals got on the ark.
Noah's Wife:	Hey, Noah, where's the swimming pool?
Noah:	It's not that kind of boat!
Noah's Wife:	Oh. Too bad.
Narrator:	At last, they were all onboard, and God shut the door.
Sound Effects:	Slam!
God:	Hey, that's my line. Slam!
Noah's Wife:	Ouch! *(Hop around on one foot.)*
Narrator:	God didn't shut the door on Noah's wife's foot!
Noah's Wife:	*(Stop hopping around.)* Oh. Too bad.
Noah:	No, it was good!
Noah's Wife:	Oh. Too good!
Narrator:	And the ark floated on the water.
Sound Effects:	Whoosh! Whoosh! Spray, spray. Whoosh! Whoosh! Splash! *(Pull out the bottle of bubbles and blow them in the face of the NARRATOR again.)*
Noah's Wife:	Whee! Whee!
Narrator:	The ark rolled back and forth on the waves.
Noah's Wife:	Uh-oh.
Narrator:	What?
Noah's Wife:	I'm getting seasick.
Sound Effects:	*(Hand her the brown lunch bag.)*
Noah's Wife:	Thanks. *(Turn your back to the audience and bend over; pretend to throw up.)*
Sound Effects:	*(Make gross throw up sounds.)*
Noah's Wife:	*(Turn and face the audience again, then say…)* Ahh…much better.

Narrator:	For a whole year they lived on that zoo cruise…with all those animals.
Sound Effects:	Snarl, snarl. Growl, growl. Hoot, hoot. Howl!
Narrator:	And they were safe.
Sound Effects:	*(Gesturing like an umpire)* Safe!
Narrator:	Finally, they landed on the side of a tall mountain.
Sound Effects:	Wham!
Narrator:	Softly.
Sound Effects:	Oh. *(Whispering)* Wham.
Noah's Wife:	C'mon everyone! Time to get out!
Sound Effects:	Snarl, snarl. Growl, growl. Hoot, hoot. Howl!
Noah:	Okay!
Narrator:	Then they sacrificed some animals.
Noah:	Let's roast 'em up!
Sound Effects:	Sizzle, sizzle. Grill, grill. Snap, crackle, pop!
Noah's Wife:	Good. I'm hungry.
Noah:	Not for us—for God! As a way of saying thanks to Him for saving us!
Narrator:	And God sent a rainbow…
Sound Effects:	Ta-da!
Narrator:	and a promise that He would never let another flood wipe out the whole world.
Sound Effects:	*(Singing majestically)* Hallelujah! Hallelujah!
Everyone:	*(Together)* The end!

(Smile, bow, and then take your seat.)

A Son for Sarah and Abraham

BASED ON: Genesis 18:1–15, 21:1–7

BIG IDEA: God kept His promise to send Abraham and Sarah a son in their old age.

BACKGROUND: God had given Abraham a number of promises including honor, land, descendants, and a future blessing. Abraham and his wife waited a long time to see God's promise of descendants come true.

Finally, God gave them a specific timeframe—within a few months Sarah would become pregnant. She found that promise unbelievable, but God fulfilled His promise, making her and everyone else who heard about it laugh for joy.

NEW TESTAMENT CONNECTION: Just like God kept His promises to Abraham and Sarah, we can count on God to keep His promises to us today (see 2 Corinthians 1:20).

All who believe are spiritual descendants of Abraham (see Galatians 3:6–9)

CAST: You'll need 5 children for this skit: Narrator (girl or boy), Sarah (preferably a girl), Abraham (preferably a boy), God (boy or girl), Baby Isaac (boy)

PROPS: Dark glasses and a baseball cap

TOPICS: Angels, babies, faith, family relationships, God's love, God's promises, listening to God, patience, prophecy fulfillment

TIPS: Since God is in disguise in this skit, you may wish to let the person playing God wear the dark glasses and the baseball cap as a disguise.

Position the Narrator and God on the left side of the stage, Abraham and Sarah in the center, and Baby Isaac on the right side of the stage next to Sarah. Bring up the stage lights, and then begin when the listeners are quiet.

A SON FOR SARAH AND ABRAHAM

DIRECTOR: Lights! Camera! Action!

NARRATOR: Abraham and his wife, Sarah, didn't have a house.

SARAH: No home sweet home.

NARRATOR: They just traveled from place to place, camping in large tents.

ABRAHAM: Just tent sweet tent.

SARAH: Let's set up camp here, Abe. What do you say?

ABRAHAM: Looks good to me, Sarah. Those oak trees will give us some good shade.

NARRATOR: One day, Abraham was sitting under one of the trees near the entrance to his tent. When he looked up, he saw three men nearby.

ABRAHAM: Howdy! Come on in, y'all!

GOD: Why, thank you.

NARRATOR: He didn't know two of them were angels and one was God Himself, in disguise.

GOD: Hee, hee, hee. That's Me.

ABRAHAM: Hey, Sarah!

SARAH: Yes, Abe?

ABRAHAM: Set out some drinks and fresh bread! We've got guests!

SARAH: Sure thing.

ABRAHAM: And let's fire up the grill and throw on some steaks. These guys look hungry!

SARAH: You got it!

NARRATOR: After that, Abraham set out some cold milk for the visitors, and they all sat down for supper.

GOD: Thanks for your hospitality, Abraham.

ABRAHAM: We aim to please.

GOD: By the way, where's your wife, Sarah?

ABRAHAM: Oh, she's in the tent.

NARRATOR: Now, Sarah wasn't exactly in the tent at the time. Instead, she was hiding nearby, listening to their conversation.

SARAH: *(Softly)* I wonder what those three men want?

GOD: Well, I've got some news for you, Abraham.

ABRAHAM: What's that?

GOD: Next year about this time, I'll return, and you two won't be alone anymore.

ABRAHAM: What do you mean? Are we gonna get a pet lizard?

GOD: No, Sarah's gonna have a baby!

NARRATOR: When Sarah heard that, she burst out laughing.

SARAH: *(Laugh, then say quietly as if you are talking to yourself…)* A baby! Yeah, right! I'm too old to have a baby. Everyone knows that!

GOD: Why did Sarah laugh? Nothing's too tough for God.

SARAH: Uh-oh.

GOD: Like I said, I'll be stopping by about this time next year, and you two are gonna have a little baby. You can count on it.

SARAH: Um, I didn't laugh.

GOD: Yes, you did.

SARAH: I did?

GOD: Yes, you laughed.

SARAH: Oopsy.

NARRATOR: Well, time passed and wouldn't you know, God's promise came true!

SARAH: *(Reach over, and pull BABY ISAAC toward you.)*

BABY ISAAC: Waa! Waa! Waa!

SARAH: Look at that! I had a baby!

ABRAHAM: Whoa. He's rather big.

SARAH:	He's a healthy baby.
BABY ISAAC:	Waa! Waa! Waa!
SARAH:	Isn't he cute? Kootchie, kootchie, koo!
ABRAHAM:	Kootchie, kootchie, koo!
BABY ISAAC:	*(Loudly)* WAA! WAA! WAA!
SARAH:	I can hardly believe I had a baby!
ABRAHAM:	You didn't believe it, remember? You laughed.
SARAH:	I didn't laugh.
ABRAHAM:	Yes, you did.
SARAH:	No, I didn't.
ABRAHAM:	Yes, you did!
SARAH:	I did?
ABRAHAM:	Yes!
SARAH:	Oopsy. Well, okay, maybe I did. But now I'm *really* laughing. *(Laugh heartily.)*
ABRAHAM:	I'll say you are.
BABY ISAAC:	Waa! Waa! Waa!
SARAH:	And I know just what we should call him—Isaac!
ABRAHAM:	Isaac? You know what that word means, don't you?
SARAH:	Yes. It means "laughter" or "joke."
ABRAHAM:	You wanna name our kid "The Joker?"
SARAH:	I wanna name him Laughter. Because at first I laughed because I doubted, and now I'm laughing because I believe!
ABRAHAM:	Oh, okay. Then his name will be Isaac!

BABY ISAAC:	Goo, goo! Gaa, gaa!
ABRAHAM:	I think he likes his name.
SARAH:	Everyone who hears about this will laugh with me. Because God brought me such joy in my old age!
GOD:	See, I told you nothing was impossible for God.
NARRATOR:	And Sarah laughed…
SARAH:	*(Laugh.)*
NARRATOR:	and Abraham laughed…
ABRAHAM:	*(Laugh.)*
NARRATOR:	and Baby Isaac laughed.
BABY ISAAC:	Waa! Waa! Waa!
NARRATOR:	Okay, so the baby cried.
BABY ISAAC:	Goo, goo! Gaa, gaa!
SARAH:	*(Sniffing the air)* That's not all he did.
ABRAHAM & SARAH:	*(Hold your noses, together)* YUCK!
BABY ISAAC:	Hee, hee, hee, hee!
NARRATOR:	And everyone who heard the story laughed too…
BABY ISAAC:	Goo, goo! Gaa, gaa!
NARRATOR:	because God had brought joy and laughter to Abraham and Sarah in their old age.
EVERYONE:	*(Together)* The end!

(Smile, bow, and then take your seat.)

GOD TESTS ABRAHAM'S FAITH

BASED ON: Genesis 22:1–19

BIG IDEA: Even though God detested human sacrifices, He ordered Abraham to sacrifice his only son as a burnt offering. Abraham was actually ready to do it when God suddenly stopped him. This test showed God Abraham's faith and resolve.

BACKGROUND: God tested Abraham's faith in a remarkable way. Abraham waited for a long time for his son Isaac to be born. Yet, when God gave him the unexpected command to kill his precious son, Abraham was ready to obey. His remarkable faith and obedience serve as an example for all believers.

NEW TESTAMENT
CONNECTION: Abraham showed extraordinary faith by sacrificing his son. (To God it was a done deal even though Abraham didn't actually kill Isaac—see Hebrews 11:8-19). Abraham believed God would raise his son from the dead because God had promised to send Abraham lots of descendants, and Abraham knew God would keep his promise, no matter what. We should follow in the footsteps of this man of faith.

Even today, all those who place their faith in God are spiritual descendants of this great man of faith (Romans 4:16–17). Also, just like God provided a ram as a substitute for Isaac, God provided Jesus as a substitute for us.

CAST: You'll need 5 children for this skit: Narrator (girl or boy), Animal (girl or boy), Isaac (boy), Abraham (boy), God (boy)

PROPS: A sign that a person can wear around her neck that says, "I'm the Donkey!" on one side and "I'm the Ram!" on the other

TOPICS: Faith, following God, God's promises, listening to God, obedience, questions

TIPS: The Animal part is purposely brief. Before the presentation, you may wish to point out to the volunteer who plays the Animal that her part is a bit shorter than the others so she doesn't feel bad when she discovers that she doesn't have as many lines as the other children. She should start the skit by wearing the sign so that the words "I'm the Donkey!" are visible to the audience.

Position the Narrator and Animal on the left side of the stage, Abraham and Isaac in the center, and God on the right side of the stage. Bring up the stage lights, and then begin when the listeners are quiet.

GOD TESTS ABRAHAM'S FAITH

DIRECTOR: Lights! Camera! Action!

NARRATOR: Abraham and his wife had waited many years to have a baby. Then one day, after their son had grown into a boy, God spoke to Abraham.

GOD: Abraham!

ABRAHAM: Yes, God. Here I am.

GOD: Take Isaac, your only son—the son you love—and go to the Mountain of Moriah.

ABRAHAM: Cool! A field trip!

GOD: It's about 50 miles from here. Then go up on the mountain…

ABRAHAM: Cool! A camping trip.

GOD: and offer him as a sacrifice to Me.

ABRAHAM: Cool! A—wait a minute! What did You say?

GOD: Offer him as a sacrifice to Me.

ABRAHAM: You mean kill him?

GOD: Uh-huh.

ABRAHAM: As in dead?

GOD: Uh-huh.

ABRAHAM: Kill my kid?

GOD: Uh-huh.

ABRAHAM: For You?

GOD: Yup. You got it.

ABRAHAM: *(Sighing)* Okay, God. Whatever You say. You're the boss.

NARRATOR: Now, God never really wanted Abraham to kill his son. He just wanted to see if Abraham would obey Him no matter what. So early the next morning, Abraham woke up his son.

ABRAHAM: Help me saddle up this donkey, Isaac.

ISAAC: Okay, Dad. This is gonna be fun! A trip to the mountains!

ANIMAL: Hee-haw.

NARRATOR: They loaded on the wood…

ANIMAL: Hee-haw. Hee-haw.

NARRATOR: and Abe and his son and a couple of his servants set off on their trip.

ANIMAL: Hee-haw. Hee-haw. Hee-haw.

NARRATOR: It took three days to get to the mountains.

ANIMAL: Hee-haw. Hee-haw. Hee-haw. Hee-haw.

NARRATOR: They left the servants with the donkey…

ANIMAL: Hee-haw.

NARRATOR: and traveled the rest of the way on foot.

ISAAC: Um, Dad?

ABRAHAM: Yes, Isaac?

ISAAC: We've got the wood here.

ABRAHAM: Uh-huh.

ISAAC: We've got a knife.

ABRAHAM: Right.

ISAAC: We've got matches to start a fire.

ABRAHAM: Yes.

ISAAC: But where's the lamb we're going to offer to God?

ABRAHAM: Well…God Himself will provide the lamb, my son.

ISAAC: Okay, Dad. Whatever you say.

NARRATOR: When they reached the place in the mountains that God had pointed out to Abraham, they stopped.

ABRAHAM: Here we are, Isaac.

ISAAC: Where's the lamb?

ABRAHAM: God will provide. Let's get set up while we wait.

NARRATOR: So they piled up the rocks, built an altar, and set out the wood.

ISAAC: I don't see any lambs, Dad.

17

ABRAHAM:	God will provide one. I promise.
NARRATOR:	Then Abe took Isaac and tied him up…
ISAAC:	Um, Dad, what are you doing? Have you lost your marbles?
NARRATOR:	and laid him on the altar.
ISAAC:	Last time I checked I'm not a lamb, Dad!
ABRAHAM:	God will provide a lamb.
ISAAC:	He'd better do it quick!
NARRATOR:	Abraham picked up the knife.
ISAAC:	That knife looks awfully pointy!
NARRATOR:	He raised the knife.
ISAAC:	*(Weakly)* Help.
NARRATOR:	When suddenly, God shouted…
GOD:	Abraham! Abraham!
ABRAHAM:	Yes, God. Here I am.
GOD:	Don't hurt him. Put down that knife. Don't lay a hand on him.
ISAAC:	Whew, baby. That was close.
GOD:	Now I know that you really do fear Me because you have offered Me your only son.
NARRATOR:	Just then, Abraham looked up and saw a ram nearby, caught in the thicket.
ANIMAL:	*(Flip your sign over so that it reads, "I'm the Ram.")* Baa, baa.
NARRATOR:	He untied Isaac.
ISAAC:	Whew.
ANIMAL:	Baa, baa…uh-oh.

NARRATOR:	And together they grabbed the ram and killed it…
ANIMAL:	Ouch.
NARRATOR:	and offered it up to God.
ANIMAL:	Sizzle. Sizzle. Sizzle.
ISAAC:	Dad, you were right! God did provide a lamb.
ABRAHAM:	I told you He would.
ISAAC:	But He cut it a little close there, don't you think?
ABRAHAM:	Isaac, God's timing is always right on the nose.
ISAAC:	Yeah, I guess you're right.
NARRATOR:	And so Abraham named that place "The Lord Will Provide."
ABRAHAM:	Let's call this place "The Lord Will Provide."
ISAAC:	Sounds good to me.
GOD:	Me too.
NARRATOR:	And since then, people have said, "On the mountain of the Lord, it will be provided."
ABRAHAM:	Because that was the day the Lord provided for me…
ISAAC:	And me…
ANIMAL:	With me. Baa, baa. Sizzle.
EVERYONE:	*(Together)* The end!

(Smile, bow, and then take your seat.)

Joseph's Journey from the Pit to the Palace

Based On: Genesis 37–50

Big Idea: Through the good times and bad times, God was working behind the scenes in Joseph's life to bring a blessing to the land.

Background: The epic tale of Joseph sweeps through more than a dozen chapters of Genesis. Through this story we see how God led His people to Egypt and then to the Promised Land. (This drama covers quite a large section of Scripture. It would make a good summary of the story of Joseph.)

New Testament Connection: Romans 8:28 (NIV) explains that God still works behind the scenes to bring blessings to His people: *And we know that in all things God works for the good of those who love him, who have been called according to his purpose.*

Cast: You'll need 5-7 children for this skit: Narrator (girl or boy), Brother (preferably a boy), Pharaoh (preferably a boy), Potiphar (preferably a boy), Wife #1 (girl), Wife #2 (girl), Joseph (boy)

Props: None (or an optional sign for Pharaoh/Potiphar)

Topics: Bullies, dreams, family relationships, following God, leadership, listening to God, perseverance, planning, questions, resentment, success, wisdom

Tips: If you don't have enough students for all of the reading parts, you could have one student play both Pharaoh and Potiphar. Make him a sign to wear around his neck that says, "I'm Potiphar!" on one side and "Now, I'm Pharaoh!" on the other. Start the skit with the Potiphar side visible to the audience. You could also use one girl to play the parts of both Wife #1 and Wife #2.

Also, if you have younger students, you may wish to explain to them that "Pharaoh" was the king of the land, or simply refer to him throughout the skit as "The King."

Position the Narrator and Joseph on the left side of the stage, the Wife/s and the Brother in the center, and Pharaoh and Potiphar on the right side of the stage. Bring up the stage lights, and then begin when the listeners are quiet.

Joseph's Journey from the Pit to the Palace

DIRECTOR: Lights! Camera! Action!

NARRATOR: Joseph had 10 older brothers who all hated him and wanted him dead.

BROTHER: Joseph's a little twerp. Let's waste him!

NARRATOR: One day, they were going to kill him… but then decided to just throw him in a pit and let him starve to death instead.

JOSEPH: How kind.

NARRATOR: However, when they saw some slave traders, they had another idea.

BROTHER: Let's sell him and make some money off him!

NARRATOR: So they pulled him up out of the pit…

JOSEPH: It was the pits in there.

NARRATOR: and sold him as a slave.

BROTHER: See ya later, Alligator!

JOSEPH: I get the feeling those guys don't like me very much.

BROTHER: You could say that again.

NARRATOR: The slave traders took Joseph to Egypt and sold him as a slave to the leader of Pharaoh's bodyguards, a man named Potiphar.

POTIPHAR: Take good care of my house, Joseph. I'm putting you in charge of everything.

JOSEPH: I will, sir.

NARRATOR: But soon after that, Potiphar's wife noticed Joseph and thought he was cute…

WIFE #1: *(Smiling)* What a hunk!

NARRATOR: and asked Joseph to make out with her.

WIFE #1: Kiss me, Big Boy!

JOSEPH: Yuck! You're already married! That's against God's rules!

NARRATOR: But she kept it up day after day.

WIFE #1: C'mon, Big Boy! Kiss me! My lips are burning for you!

JOSEPH: You're being very gross—do you know that?

NARRATOR: Until finally, Joseph ran away from her, and she got him in trouble with her husband.

POTIPHAR: Why were you trying to kiss my wife?

JOSEPH: I wasn't! Honest! Trust me!

NARRATOR: But Potiphar didn't listen to Joseph. Instead, he listened to his wife.

POTIPHAR: I'm throwing you in the slammer.

JOSEPH: I was afraid of that.

WIFE #1: Bye-bye, Big Boy.

NARRATOR: Joseph spent more than two years in jail.

JOSEPH: Things just aren't going my way.

NARRATOR: But God was with Joseph, and one day the king had two dreams that nobody could figure out.

PHARAOH: *(If you are using the sign, flip it so that it reads, "Now, I'm Pharaoh!")* Can't anybody tell me what my dreams mean?

NARRATOR: Someone remembered that Joseph could interpret dreams, so he was brought quickly to the palace to help the king.

PHARAOH: Okay, Joseph! Explain my dreams!

JOSEPH: I can't do that, your majesty. But God can. He'll explain 'em to me and I'll explain 'em to you.

PHARAOH: Funky.

NARRATOR: And it happened just like Joseph said. Pharaoh told Joseph about the dreams, and Joseph explained that there would be 7 years of good weather.

PHARAOH: That's good.

JOSEPH: And 7 years of bad weather.

PHARAOH: That's bad. What should we do—move to Florida?

20

JOSEPH: No, find someone smart to lead the people. Then have that person save up lots of food during the good years to eat during the bad years.

PHARAOH: Hmm... What are you doing for the next 14 years?

JOSEPH: Not much.

PHARAOH: You got the job.

JOSEPH: Thanks.

NARRATOR: So when Joseph was 30 years old…

JOSEPH: Happy Birthday to me!

NARRATOR: he became the leader of the land, answering only to Pharaoh.

PHARAOH: Here are lots of riches for you…

JOSEPH: Cool.

PHARAOH: and a wife!

WIFE #2: Kiss me, Big Boy.

JOSEPH: Oh, no! Not again!

NARRATOR: And after the 7 years of good weather…

PHARAOH: Ah!

NARRATOR: came the 7 years of bad weather.

PHARAOH: Yuck!

NARRATOR: Egypt was the only place with any food. Joseph's brothers needed food, so they went down to Egypt.

BROTHER: I'm starving! I hope they have a burger joint down there!

NARRATOR: Well, they didn't know that the guy handing out food was their long lost brother. But when they arrived, Joseph recognized them.

JOSEPH: Whoa, baby, it's my brothers! The ones who stuck me in that pit to kill me! That was the pits.

NARRATOR: Now, Joseph wasn't sure if he could trust his brothers after all those years. So after a bunch of tests, he finally broke down and cried.

BROTHER: Why is that guy crying?

JOSEPH: It's me…Joseph! Your long lost brother!

BROTHER: Whoa, baby.

NARRATOR: Joseph invited the whole family to live with him, and they all moved to Egypt.

BROTHER: Oh, goody! Can we visit the pyramids?

JOSEPH: No.

BROTHER: Oh. Okay.

NARRATOR: As time passed, the brothers became more and more scared. They thought Joseph would try to get back at them because they had been so mean to him a long time ago.

BROTHER: Oh, Joseph, please don't hurt us!

JOSEPH: I won't.

BROTHER: You mean you're not mad?

JOSEPH: Not anymore.

BROTHER: Are you gonna try to get back at us?

JOSEPH: No. What you guys meant for bad, God used for good.

BROTHER: Is this some kind of a trick?

JOSEPH: Nope.

BROTHER: Whoa, baby.

JOSEPH: It's not a trick. It's called love.

BROTHER: I thought it was called Egypt?

JOSEPH: I'm saying, I love you and I forgive you.

BROTHER: Oh. Cool. That's so sweet! Kiss me, Big Boy!

JOSEPH: No thanks.

NARRATOR: And so, Joseph took care of his brothers and was kind to them and to their families from then on.

EVERYONE: *(Together)* The end!

(Smile, bow, and then take your seat.)

God Makes Walls Fall at Jericho

BASED ON: Joshua 6:12–21

BIG IDEA: God knocked down the walls of Jericho and handed the Israelites a great victory on their quest to conquer the Promised Land.

BACKGROUND: Jericho was an ancient city that had stood for thousands of years. Many people thought it was invincible. It had walls that were up to 20 feet thick and more than 20 feet tall, so when God led Joshua and the children of Israel into the Promised Land, one of the first tasks was to conquer Jericho. God's unusual battle strategy proved to everyone, including the Israelites, that God was powerful enough to deliver them from any enemy.

NEW TESTAMENT CONNECTION: Today, Christians don't typically have to battle against reinforced cities, but we do have a strong spiritual foe who is out to get us (see Ephesians 6:12). And, just like the Israelites, our victory comes through our faith in God rather than our own schemes and ideas.

CAST: You'll need 5-9 children for this skit: Narrator (girl or boy), 1-3 Citizens of Jericho (girls or boys), 1-3 Soldiers (boys or girls), Joshua (preferably a boy), God (boy)

PROPS: Large cardboard boxes to represent the walls of Jericho (optional)

TOPICS: Faith, following God, God's power, God's promises, leadership, listening to God, obedience

TIPS: You may wish to have the students act out parts of this story. If so, practice before your presentation so the children are confident enough to know what to say, what to do, and where to stand or move.

If you use more than one Soldier, have one of them be the spokesperson and have the others only join in by saying certain words of phrases. In their scripts, highlight only the words you want them to read.

Position Joshua and the Soldiers on the left side of the stage, God and the Narrator in the center, and the Citizens of Jericho on the right side of the stage. You may wish to have God stand on a chair or stool. If you use cardboard boxes to represent the walls of Jericho, position them between the Citizens and other readers in center stage. Bring up the stage lights, and then begin when the listeners are quiet.

GOD MAKES WALLS FALL AT JERICHO

DIRECTOR: Lights! Camera! Action!

NARRATOR: Jericho was a great big city with tall, tall walls.

SOLDIER: *(Look up toward the CITIZENS OF JERICHO.)* Whoa. Those walls are tall!

CITIZENS: Our walls are tall!
Our walls won't fall!
You can't dent our walls at all!
Naa-naa-nah-boo-boo! *(Stick out your tongue.)*

NARRATOR: But then God spoke to Joshua.

GOD: Josh, I'm giving you this city.

JOSHUA: *(Look up toward GOD.)* Cool.

GOD: Here's what to do. Get a bunch of trumpets and then march around the city.

JOSHUA: You want a marching band?

GOD: Something like that. Toot the trumpets the whole time.

JOSHUA: That's a lot of tooting.

GOD: Yup, it sure is…. Then march around the city once a day for 6 days.

JOSHUA: That's a lot of marching.

GOD: Yup, it sure is…. On the 7th day march around the city 7 times. And then I want all 600,000 of you to scream at the top of your lungs.

JOSHUA: That's a lot of noise.

GOD: Yup, it sure is…. Then I'll knock down the walls, and you can wipe out the city.

JOSHUA: That's cool.

GOD: Yup, it sure is.

NARRATOR: But the people in Jericho weren't about to give up.

CITIZENS: Our walls are tall!
Our walls won't fall!
You can't dent our walls at all!
Naa-naa-nah-boo-boo! *(Stick out your tongue.)*

NARRATOR: So Joshua told the priests the plan, and he handed out trumpets. Then they took the ark—

JOSHUA: That's a lot of animals!

NARRATOR: Um…not that ark. The Ark of the Covenant. The one with God's laws in it.

JOSHUA: Oh, yeah. Right.

NARRATOR: And then the soldiers and priests marched around the city.

SOLDIER: *(Chanting and marching like a soldier. If you are acting out the story, the SOLDIERS can march around the audience.)* Left…left… left, right, left! Left…left…left, right, left!

NARRATOR: Um. They were quiet as they marched.

SOLDIER: Oh. *(Mouthing the words and marching)* Left…left…left, right, left! Left…left…left, right, left!

NARRATOR: They did this for 6 days…

SOLDIER: *(Talking very fast)* Left…left…left, right, left! Left…left…left, right, left!

NARRATOR: while the people in Jericho watched from the top of the walls.

CITIZENS: Our walls are tall!
Our walls won't fall!
You can't dent our walls at all!
Naa-naa-nah-boo-boo! *(Stick out your tongue.)*

NARRATOR: On the 7th day they marched around the city 7 times, just as God had said.

SOLDIER: Oh, boy, here we go. *(Acting really tired)* Left…left…left, right, left! Left…left…left, right, left! Whew! That's a lot of marching.

GOD: Yup, it sure is.

NARRATOR: Then the soldiers were quiet while the priests blew their trumpets. *(Wait… Nothing happens. Then say to the SOLDIER…)* I said the priests blew their trumpets.

SOLDIER: I know. I'm a soldier, remember?

23

NARRATOR: Blow a trumpet already! We don't have anyone playing the priests.

SOLDIER: Oh. Okay. Where's my trumpet?

NARRATOR: Use your imagination.

SOLDIER: Oh. Okay. *(Pretending to blow a trumpet)* Toot...toot...toot, toot, toot! Toot...toot...toot, toot, toot!

NARRATOR: Very nice. And then Josh said…

JOSHUA: Okay, it's time to shout like you mean it!

NARRATOR: And the soldiers and priests all shouted—

SOLDIER: Like you mean it!

NARRATOR: No, that's not what I meant! I meant they shouted loudly!

SOLDIER: Oh. Loudly!

NARRATOR: Just shout already!

SOLDIER: Already!

NARRATOR: *(Sigh.)*

SOLDIER: Timber?

NARRATOR: Well, close enough. And then the walls came down!

(GOD, step off your chair or stool, walk over, and knock the walls down. If you are using cardboard boxes to represent the walls, knock them over and throw a few at the people hiding behind them.)

CITIZENS: Our walls are tall! Our walls won't fall! You can't dent our— *(Pause and look up as if seeing the walls falling on top of you.)*

Uh-oh…. Our walls *were* tall! Our walls *did* fall! And they basically smashed us as flat as a pancake.

NARRATOR: And the soldiers and priests and Joshua went in and killed the people of the city. *(You could act this part out if you like.)*

CITIZENS: Agh! Help! *(Fall over and act dead.)*

JOSHUA: That's a lot of dead people.

GOD: Yup, it sure is.

SOLDIER: Hooray!...Hooray!... Hooray, hooray, hooray!

Hooray!...Hooray!... Hooray, hooray, hooray!

NARRATOR: The Israelites trusted God, they did what He said, and God kept His promises to them!

GOD: Yup, I sure did.

EVERYONE: *(Together)* The end!

(Smile, bow, and then take your seat.)

Naomi's New Family

BASED ON:

Ruth 1–4

BIG IDEA:

Naomi's life seemed empty and bitter until God brought her a new family and great joy.

BACKGROUND:

The days of the Judges were marked by moral and spiritual decay in Israel. However, there were still periods of peace and people of faith. This story occurs during that time and provides examples for us of God's faithfulness and Ruth's faithfulness.

When Naomi's husband and two sons died, she became bitter. But God filled her life with joy and a new family through her young daughter-in-law's marriage with the kindly Boaz.

NEW TESTAMENT

CONNECTION:

Ruth, a lady from Moab, believed in the God of Israel. God's love and forgiveness are for all people regardless of their background, lineage, or ethnicity (see Acts 10:34-35). Also, Boaz "redeems" Ruth and shows us a picture of Christ's redeeming work for His own bride, the Church (see Galatians 4:5 and Titus 2:14).

CAST:

You'll need 8 children for this skit: Narrator #1 (girl or boy), Narrator #2 (girl or boy), Ruth (preferably a girl), Naomi (preferably a girl), Boaz (preferably a boy), Elimelech (boy), Mahlon (boy), Kilion (boy)

PROPS:

None

TOPICS:

Anger, faithfulness, family relationships, God's sovereignty, grief and loss, loneliness, patience, questions, second chances, suffering

TIPS:

The three boys don't have long speaking parts, but they do have fun parts. Select some boys who like to ham it up!

Position the Narrators next to each other; Ruth, Boaz, and Naomi next to each other; and the other three boys next to each other. Bring up the stage lights, and then begin when the listeners are quiet.

Naomi's New Family

DIRECTOR: Lights! Camera! Action!

NARRATOR #1: Back when there were Judges in Israel…

NARRATOR #2: That's the ruler-kind of Judges, not the Court TV-kind of judges.

NARRATOR #1: a man left Bethlehem with his family and traveled to Moab where there was more food.

ELIMELECH: There's gotta be a grocery store around here somewhere!

MAHLON: Dad, are we there yet?

KILION: I gotta go to the bathroom!

NAOMI: Quiet, kids. Your dad is trying to drive!

NARRATOR #2: But then he died.

ELIMELECH: *(Draw your finger across your throat, stick out your tongue and act dead.)* **Agh!**

NARRATOR #1: His sons grew up, got married, and then they died, too.

MAHLON: *(Draw your finger across your throat, stick out your tongue and act dead.)* **Agh!**

KILION: *(Draw your finger across your throat, stick out your tongue and act dead.)* **Agh!**

NARRATOR #2: Naomi, their mother, was all alone.

NAOMI: I'm gonna go back to Bethlehem. There are too many people dying around here.

ELIMELECH: *(Die again.)* **Agh!**

MAHLON: *(Die again.)* **Agh!**

KILION: *(Die again.)* **Agh!**

NARRATOR #1: One of her sons had married a woman from Moab named Ruth.

RUTH: I wish my hubby hadn't died.

KILION: *(Die again.)* **Agh!**

NARRATOR #2: So when Naomi returned to Bethlehem, Ruth decided to go with her.

RUTH: Your land will be my land. Your people will be my people. And your God will be my God.

NARRATOR #1: When they arrived in Bethlehem, everyone started talking about them.

(During this exchange, the NARRATORS address each other rather than the audience.)

NARRATOR #2: Can you believe Naomi is back?

NARRATOR #1: Is it really her?

NARRATOR #2: I heard it is.

NARRATOR #1: But could it really be her after all these years?

NAOMI: It's me but don't call me Naomi anymore. That's a pretty name that means "pleasant," but I'm not feeling pleasant at all. My husband died…

ELIMELECH: *(Die again.)* **Agh!**

NAOMI: and then my two sons died.

MAHLON: *(Die again.)* **Agh!**

KILION: *(Die again.)* **Agh!**

NAOMI: So from now on call me Mara.

NARRATOR #2: But Mara means "bitter"!

NAOMI: I know. God has made my life bitter. I went away full, but when my husband died…

ELIMELECH: *(Die again.)* **Agh!**

NAOMI: and my two sons died…

MAHLON: *(Die again.)* **Agh!**

KILION: *(Die again.)* **Agh!**

NAOMI: my life became empty.

NARRATOR #1: *(To NARRATOR #2)* She's got issues.

NARRATOR #2: *(To NARRATOR #1)* I'll say.

NARRATOR #1: So Naomi and Ruth arrived in Bethlehem at the start of the barley harvest.

NARRATOR #2: Now, a man was living there named Boaz.

BOAZ: Hey, everyone! That's me!

NARRATOR #1: He was very friendly.

BOAZ: *(Go around the audience shaking people's hands and greeting them, saying things like, "So glad to meet you!" "Really, it's a pleasure!" "Very nice shirt you have on there!" "Have a wonderful day!")*

NARRATOR #2: And he loved God.

BOAZ: Praise the Lord and Hallelujah! Amen and Amen!

NARRATOR #1: Then he saw Ruth.

BOAZ: Whoa, baby. Who's that?

NARRATOR #2: The men in the field told him it was Ruth, the lady from Moab.

BOAZ: Listen, Ruth.

RUTH: Yes?

BOAZ: Whenever you or Naomi—I mean Mara—need food, come here to my field.

RUTH: Thank you.

BOAZ: Don't worry—no one will hurt you.

RUTH: Okay.

BOAZ: And if you get thirsty, just go get a drink from the water jars.

RUTH: Well, thanks!

NARRATOR #1: Ruth was amazed by his kindness.

RUTH: Why are you being so nice?

BOAZ: I think you're cute.

NARRATOR #1: Um, he didn't say that.

BOAZ: Oh, yeah. *(Clear your throat.)* I heard you helped care for Naomi—I mean Mara—after your husband died…

KILION: *(Die again.)* Agh!

BOAZ: and his brother and his dad died, too…

MAHLON: *(Die again.)* Agh!

ELIMELECH: *(Die again.)* Agh!

BOAZ: and I'm praying that God will show you His kindness because you showed kindness to Naomi—I mean Mara…

RUTH: Thank you.

BOAZ: and I think you're cute.

NARRATOR #1: Um, he didn't say that.

BOAZ: Oh.

NARRATOR #2: Then he invited her over for supper.

NARRATOR #1: And he told his farm workers to leave extra barley out for her to gather.

NAOMI: Where did you get all this barley?

RUTH: A guy named Boaz.

NAOMI: I think he likes you.

RUTH: Why do you say that?

NAOMI: When a guy gives a girl this much barley, he likes her. Trust me.

RUTH: And he invited me back to his fields.

NAOMI: I'll bet he thinks you're cute!

BOAZ: I do.

NARRATOR #2: *(Clear your throat.)* Eh-hem… So one day Naomi had an idea.

NAOMI: Um, Ruth?

RUTH: Yes?

NAOMI: Tonight put on your prettiest dress and go meet Boaz. It's time to go on a date.

RUTH: Okay.

NARRATOR #1: So that night, Boaz fell asleep by the barley field. When he woke up, there was a woman lying there by his feet.

BOAZ: Whoa, baby.

RUTH: Hi.

BOAZ: Who are you?

RUTH: It's me, Ruth!

BOAZ: Oh.

RUTH: Wanna get married?

BOAZ: Okay.

NARRATOR #2: Then he gave her six scoops of barley, and she went home to Naomi.

NAOMI: Well, how'd it go?

RUTH: Pretty good, I guess. Look at all this barley he gave me!

27

NAOMI: Honey, this guy is smitten. By the end of the day, wedding bells are gonna chime!

NARRATOR #1: So Boaz planned the wedding, and soon they were married.

(ELIMELECH, MAHLON, and KILION hum "Here Comes the Bride.")

NARRATOR #2: Soon they had a baby boy.

BOAZ: That was fast.

RUTH: I've been pregnant for 9 months, Boaz.

BOAZ: Oh, yeah. I forgot.

NARRATOR #1: And the women of the town all went to Naomi and said, "Look! God has given Ruth a baby, and you can help raise him!"

NAOMI: Yeah, I guess so.

NARRATOR #2: So your life's not empty any more!

NAOMI: I guess not!

NARRATOR #1: Naomi helped care for the baby as if he were her own son, even though, of course, her sons were dead…

MAHLON: *(Die again.)* Agh!

KILION: *(Die again.)* Agh!

NARRATOR #2: and so was her husband.

ELIMELECH: *(Die again.)* Agh!

NARRATOR #1: And when that little baby grew up, he became the grandpa of King David.

NARRATOR #2: And an ancestor of another famous baby—

EVERYONE: *(Together)* JESUS!

NARRATOR #1: And after that, Ruth and Boaz lived happily ever after.

EVERYONE: *(Together)* The end!

(Smile, bow, and then take your seat.)

Samuel and the Voice in the Night

Based On: 1 Samuel 3

Big Idea: Samuel learned to listen to God's voice and share what God had to say. He became one of God's greatest spokespersons.

Background: Samuel was the long-awaited son of a prayerful woman named Hannah. Since she had promised to dedicate him to the Lord, she took him to the worship tent while he was still a young boy, and he began to live there. Samuel helped the aging priest Eli with the chores since his eyesight was failing.

God had warned Eli that he should do a better job of disciplining his sons, or there would be severe consequences (1 Samuel 2:27-36). Then one night God spoke to Samuel and, after some confusion about who was talking to him, he listened. The next morning he delivered God's word to Eli, even though he knew it was news Eli wouldn't want to hear. Consequently, Samuel became one of God's most trusted and faithful prophets.

New Testament Connection: When we hear God speak to us through the Bible, we should listen and obey as well. And we should tell others what God has to say, even if it's news they might not want to hear: *We cannot help speaking about what we have seen and heard* (Acts 4:20, NIV).

Cast: You'll need 4-5 children for this skit: 1-2 Narrators (girls or boys), Eli (preferably a boy), Samuel (preferably a boy), God (boy)

Props: None

Topics: Calling, consequences, family relationships, following God, God's Word, leadership, listening to God, obedience

Tips: You can have two Narrators for this drama, or you may choose to just have one child read all of the Narrators' parts.

Position Eli on the opposite side of the stage from Samuel. Throughout the skit, whenever Samuel runs over to talk with Eli, he has to cross the entire stage! God and the Narrator can be positioned in center stage. Bring up the stage lights, and then begin when the listeners are quiet.

SAMUEL AND THE VOICE IN THE NIGHT

DIRECTOR: Lights! Camera! Action!

NARRATOR #1: When Samuel was a boy, a priest named Eli took care of him.

NARRATOR #2: And Samuel helped Eli with his work since Eli didn't have very good eyesight.

ELI: Time for beddy-bye, Samuel!

SAMUEL: Can't I stay up a little later? Please? Pretty please?

ELI: Nope. Now go to bed.

NARRATOR #1: In those days, God didn't reveal Himself to His people very often. Messages from God were very rare.

ELI: Nighty-night, Samuel!

SAMUEL: Nighty-night, Eli.

NARRATOR #2: That night, the lamps were burning and everyone was in bed, when suddenly Samuel heard his name.

GOD: Samuel! Samuel!

NARRATOR #1: Samuel got up and ran to Eli.

SAMUEL: *(Run across the stage to ELI.)* Yes, here I am. What is it, Eli?

NARRATOR #1: He thought it was Eli since he was the only other person there.

SAMUEL: I heard you calling. What do you want?

ELI: *(Yawning)* I didn't call you, Samuel. I've been asleep. You're probably imagining things. Now go back to bed.

SAMUEL: Okay. *(Go back to the other side of the stage.)*

NARRATOR #2: So Samuel crawled back into bed and closed his eyes.

GOD: Samuel! Samuel!

SAMUEL: Not this again!

NARRATOR #1: Samuel got up and ran to Eli.

SAMUEL: *(Run across the stage to ELI.)* Yes, what do you want, Eli? I heard you calling me.

ELI: I didn't call you, my boy. Now go to sleep.

SAMUEL: But—

ELI: Go on.

SAMUEL: I'm telling you I heard my name!

ELI: You're just dreaming. Now goodnight.

SAMUEL: *(Sighing)* Oh, okay. Goodnight.

NARRATOR #2: So Samuel went back to bed.

SAMUEL: *(Walk back across the stage.)*

GOD: Samuel! Samuel!

SAMUEL: *(To NARRATOR #1)* Lemme guess, Samuel got up and ran to Eli.

NARRATOR #1: Yup.

SAMUEL: I thought so. *(Hop up and run across the stage to ELI.)* Yes, Eli? What is it?

ELI: What are you talking about?

SAMUEL: I heard you calling my name!

ELI: Wait a minute! We're the only ones here, right?

SAMUEL: Right.

ELI: And you keep hearing someone call your name right?

SAMUEL: That's right.

ELI: And it's not me—

SAMUEL: So you say.

ELI: That leaves only one option!

SAMUEL: Someone left the TV on?

ELI: No.

SAMUEL: Ghosts?

ELI: No, of course not! God!

SAMUEL: God?

ELI: Yes! He's speaking to you. Go back to bed and listen. If you hear the voice again, say, "Speak to me Lord. I'm ready to listen." Got it?

SAMUEL: Speak to me Lord. I'm ready to listen.

ELI:	Right. Say that if the voice comes back.
SAMUEL:	You're sure it's not you?
ELI:	Positive.
SAMUEL:	I'm not on Candid Camera or anything, am I?
ELI:	No. Now go to bed. And what are you gonna say if you hear the voice again?
SAMUEL:	Speak to me, Lord. I'm ready to listen.
ELI:	Right. Now goodnight.
SAMUEL:	Goodnight.
NARRATOR #2:	So Samuel went back to bed, lay down, and waited.
SAMUEL:	*(Walk back across the stage.)*
NARRATOR #1:	Before that night, he had never heard God speak to him. But pretty soon Samuel heard the voice again.
GOD:	Samuel! Samuel!
SAMUEL:	Okay, let's see, how did that go again? Oh, yeah.... Speak to me, Lord. I'm ready to listen.
GOD:	I'm going to do something that will shake up everyone in Israel. I warned Eli about letting his sons insult Me and disobey Me, but he didn't even try to stop them.
SAMUEL:	*(To the audience)* Yikes. He sounds mad.
GOD:	Well, his time is up. This is my message—Eli's family has sins that are never going to get washed away.
SAMUEL:	Whoa. That's some message.
GOD:	That's all for now.... Nighty-night, Samuel!
SAMUEL:	Nighty-night, God.
NARRATOR #2:	Samuel just lay there until morning. Finally, he got up and started his work, opening the doors and getting everything ready for the worship service.
NARRATOR #1:	But he dreaded the thought of telling Eli about the vision.
SAMUEL:	What's he gonna do to me if I tell him?
NARRATOR #2:	Then Eli woke up.

ELI:	Samuel! Samuel!
SAMUEL:	Oh, no. Not this again. Speak to me, Lord. I'm ready to listen—
ELI:	No, no, no. It's me this time. It's Eli!
SAMUEL:	Oh. What can I do for you, Eli?
ELI:	Well, what did God say to you? Tell me everything!
SAMUEL:	Everything?
ELI:	Yup. Word for word.
SAMUEL:	Are you sure you don't want to hear the Reader's Digest condensed version?
ELI:	No, word for word.
SAMUEL:	Okay, here goes....
NARRATOR #1:	And Samuel told Eli everything God had said to him.
ELI:	Hmm. God said that?
SAMUEL:	Yup.
ELI:	Well...He's God. Let Him do what He thinks is best.
NARRATOR #2:	So Samuel grew up, and God continued to speak to him.
GOD:	Samuel! Samuel!
SAMUEL:	Yes, God?
GOD:	I've got another message for you.
SAMUEL:	Speak to me, Lord. I'm ready to listen!
NARRATOR #1:	And Samuel told the people whatever God said.
NARRATOR #2:	He spoke God's word to them from one end of the country to the other.
NARRATOR #1:	He never backed down.
NARRATOR #2:	And everyone could tell he was a true prophet of God.
GOD:	Nighty-night, Samuel!
SAMUEL:	Nighty-night, God.
EVERYONE:	*(Together)* The end!

(Smile, bow, and then take your seat.)

31

DAVID AND THE GIANT PROBLEM

BASED ON: 1 Samuel 17:1–52

BIG IDEA: David placed his faith and his life in God's hands when he faced the giant Philistine, Goliath. God gave him the victory, and God gives us the victory over the giant problems in our lives too.

BACKGROUND: Under King Saul, the Israelites were facing their dreaded enemies, the Philistines. The only problem was, no one in the Israelite army (including Saul) was brave enough to fight against the Philistine champion, Goliath. Then David, a young shepherd, stepped up to the challenge armed only with a slingshot, a shepherd's staff, and an unyielding faith in God. Through David, God delivered His people from the Philistines and gave them the victory.

NEW TESTAMENT CONNECTION: God is on our side today, just like He was on David's side long ago: *If God is for us, who can be against us?* (Romans 8:31, NIV). Also, we can learn humility from David's example of giving all the credit for his victory to God.

CAST: You'll need 6-12 children for this skit: Narrator (girl or boy), 1-4 Philistines (preferably girls), 1-4 Israelites (preferably boys), David (preferably a boy), Goliath (preferably a boy), Jesse (preferably a boy)

PROPS: A chair or stool for Goliath to stand on (optional)

TOPICS: Bullies, conviction, courage, David, doubt, faith, God's power, leadership, success

TIPS: You could delete the part of Jesse if you wish to use fewer readers. You could also act out this drama as it's read. Just coach the readers on what to do and where to move.

Position the Philistines on the left side of the stage, the Israelites on the right side of the stage, the Narrator and Goliath in the center, and David and Jesse on the far right. Bring up the stage lights, and then begin when the listeners are quiet.

*This script first appeared in the 2000 Children's Ministry Seminar, "Seven Secrets to Successful Storytelling" published by the International Network of Children's Ministries. Copyright 2000. All rights reserved. Used by permission.

DAVID AND THE GIANT PROBLEM

DIRECTOR: Lights! Camera! Action!

NARRATOR: Long ago, the Israelites gathered to fight against the mighty Philistine warriors.

PHILISTINES: *(Together)* Goliath! Goliath! He's our man! If he can't do it, no one can. Goooo...Goliath!

NARRATOR: Well, if nothing else, they were pretty good cheerleaders.

PHILISTINES: *(Together)* Thank you!

NARRATOR: Anyway, the Israelites were on one hill, and the Philistines were on another. Every day the biggest, strongest, nastiest smelling warrior of the Philistines, a giant named Goliath, mocked the Israelites and their God.

GOLIATH: You measly little worms! I could fight your whole army with my pinky finger! You serve a wimpy king and a wimpy God, and you're all a bunch of chickens! Bawk! Bawk! Bawk!

PHILISTINES: *(Together)* Goliath! Goliath! He's our man! If he can't do it, no one can. Goooo...Goliath!

NARRATOR: The Israelites were terrified!

ISRAELITES: *(Chew fingers and shake knees.)*

NARRATOR: Every morning and evening for 40 days, the giant would laugh at the Israelites.

GOLIATH: *(Laugh loudly at the scared Israelites.)*

NARRATOR: The Israelites would shake on the hill, scared to death...

ISRAELITES: *(Chew fingers and shake knees.)*

NARRATOR: while the Philistines cheered on their hero.

PHILISTINES: *(Together)* Goliath! Goliath! He's our man! If he can't do it, no one can. Goooo...Goliath!

NARRATOR: One day, a young shepherd named David was sent by his father to take food to his brothers who were fighting in the war.

JESSE: Dave, take this food to your brothers who are fighting in the war.

DAVID: Sure thing, Dad.

NARRATOR: But when David arrived, he didn't see anyone fighting at all. Instead, he found the Israelites shaking and scared.

ISRAELITES: *(Chew fingers and shake knees.)*

DAVID: What's going on here? I thought you were supposed to be fighting the Philistines?

ISRAELITES: *(Together)* NO WAY!

PHILISTINES: *(Together)* Goliath! Goliath! He's our man! If he can't do it, no one can. Goooo...Goliath!

DAVID: Well...then I'll fight him. I'm not afraid of anyone as long as God is on my side!

ISRAELITES: *(Together)* David! David! He's our man! If he can't do it, we're all dead meat!

NARRATOR: The king wished David the best. And David, armed only with a slingshot and a big stick, approached the giant.

GOLIATH: Woof, woof, woof! What do I look like—a doggie, that you come at me with a stick? Here, fetch, Rover! I'm gonna step all over you! Prepare to be toe-jam!

DAVID: Not a chance, Goliath. You see, my God is a lot bigger than you, and today everyone is gonna find out just how powerful He is when I cut you down to size!

NARRATOR: David ran toward the giant and slung a stone at him. It hit the giant in the forehead and knocked him to the ground.

GOLIATH: Ouch.

NARRATOR: Then David took Goliath's own spear and sliced off his head.

GOLIATH: Yuck.

NARRATOR: Blood spewed all over, and it was really gross.

ISRAELITES: *(Together)* EW! THAT'S GROSS!

NARRATOR: The Philistines saw it and were so scared they ran for their lives...

PHILISTINES: *(Together)* Goliath! Goliath!
He's our—uh-oh.
We're outta here!

NARRATOR: being chased by the now-brave Israelites.

ISRAELITES: *(Together, flex muscles and act brave.)*

NARRATOR: And from then on, everyone knew that the God of the Israelites was for real.

EVERYONE: *(Together)* The end!

(Smile, bow, and then take your seat.)

34

SOLOMON'S RADICAL WISDOM

BASED ON: 1 Kings 3, 4:29–34 (see also 2 Chronicles 1:1–13)

BIG IDEA: When Solomon was faced with a difficult decision about the identity of a newborn baby, he showed that God had indeed given him great wisdom.

BACKGROUND: Before David died, he appointed Solomon to be the next king of Israel. Early in Solomon's reign, God asked him what gift he would like. Solomon chose a wise and discerning heart to govern the Israelites. (Note: Solomon didn't just ask for wisdom but for discernment in order to lead justly). God was pleased with Solomon's choice and gave him even more than he asked for.

In this story, two women (who were both prostitutes) claim that a baby is theirs. Solomon orders that the baby be cut in half with a sword and, based on the reaction of the two women, discerns who the true mother is. As a result of this decision, news of Solomon's great wisdom spreads throughout the land.

NEW TESTAMENT CONNECTION: When Solomon was granted a unique opportunity to ask God for a special gift, he chose wisdom. God still grants wisdom to all believers who ask for it: *If any of you lacks wisdom, you should ask God, who gives generously to all without finding fault, and it will be given to you* (James 1:5, NIV).

CAST: You'll need 6-7 children for this skit: Narrator (girl or boy), Woman #1 (girl), Woman #2 (girl), Solomon (preferably a boy), Soldier (preferably a boy), Baby (preferably a boy), God (boy)

PROPS: A fake sword and a baby boy doll (all optional)

TOPICS: Choices, giftedness, leadership, lying, prayer, success, wisdom

TIPS: You can use either a doll for the Baby, or you could use a real person. Woman #1 begins with the Baby. Give the sword to the Soldier.

Position the Women next to each other on the left side of the stage. (If you use a live person as the Baby, then position that person next to the Women.) Place Solomon and the Soldier next to each other in the center, and the Narrator and God on the right side of the stage.

Bring up the stage lights, and then begin when the listeners are quiet.

Solomon's Radical Wisdom

DIRECTOR:	Lights! Camera! Action!
NARRATOR:	When Solomon became king, he had a special time of prayer. That night, God spoke to him.
GOD:	Solomon, ask for anything you'd like and I'll give it to you!
SOLOMON:	Hmm…well, let's see. Leading all these people is a tough job.
GOD:	Yes, it is.
SOLOMON:	Please give me lots of wisdom, God, so I can tell right from wrong and make good decisions!
GOD:	Good choice.
SOLOMON:	Thank you.
GOD:	I'll also bless you with honor and riches because you made such a good choice.
SOLOMON:	Cool.
GOD:	And, if you keep my rules like your dad, King David, you'll get a nice long life too.
SOLOMON:	Well, thank you.
GOD:	You're welcome.
NARRATOR:	When Solomon woke up, he realized it had been a dream.
SOLOMON:	God spoke to me in a dream! Let's have a party and celebrate!
NARRATOR:	So Solomon worshiped God and threw a big party. Then, one day, some women came to Solomon with a problem.
SOLDIER:	Your majesty, there are two women here to see you.
SOLOMON:	Show them in.
WOMAN #1:	O King, we live together in the same house.
SOLOMON:	That's nice.
WOMAN #1:	Well, not long ago I had a baby. *(Hold up the BABY.)*
SOLOMON:	Congratulations.
WOMAN #1:	Thank you. And a few days later, she had a baby too.
SOLOMON:	Congratulations to you too.
WOMAN #2:	Thank you.
WOMAN #1:	So we were all alone in the house one night. And while we were asleep, she rolled over and killed her baby.
WOMAN #2:	Did not! *(Take the BABY.)*
WOMAN #1:	Did too! *(Take the BABY.)*
WOMAN #2:	Did not! *(Take the BABY.)*
WOMAN #1:	Did too! *(Take the BABY.)*
SOLOMON:	Now hold on there! Stop arguing. Finish your story.
WOMAN #1:	Well, during the night, she switched the babies! *(Hand the BABY to WOMAN #2.)* She put the dead baby next to me and she took my baby to keep for herself!
WOMAN #2:	Did not! *(Take the BABY.)*
WOMAN #1:	Did too! *(Take the BABY.)*
WOMAN #2:	Did not! *(Take the BABY.)*
WOMAN #1:	Did too! *(Take the BABY.)*
SOLOMON:	Stop it! What happened then?
WOMAN #1:	Well, when I woke up, I noticed that the baby next to me was dead! I thought it was mine, but when I looked closely, I realized it wasn't my baby at all! That's when I knew she'd switched 'em!
WOMAN #2:	Did not! *(Take the BABY.)*
WOMAN #1:	Did too! *(Take the BABY.)*
WOMAN #2:	Did not! *(Take the BABY.)*
WOMAN #1:	Did too! *(Take the BABY.)*
WOMAN #2:	SHE'S the one who switched 'em! *(Take the BABY.)*
WOMAN #1:	Am not! *(Take the BABY.)*
WOMAN #2:	Are too! *(Take the BABY.)*
WOMAN #1:	Am not! *(Take the BABY.)*

WOMAN #2:	**Are too!** *(Take the BABY.)*
WOMAN #1:	**No, no, NO! The DEAD baby is yours, and the LIVE one is mine!** *(Take the BABY.)*
WOMAN #2:	**Is not!** *(Take the BABY.)*
WOMAN #1:	**Is too!** *(Take the BABY.)*
WOMAN #2:	**Is not!** *(Take the BABY.)*
WOMAN #1:	**Is too!** *(Take the BABY.)*
SOLOMON:	**Quiet down, ladies!**
SOLDIER:	**You heard the king. Quiet down!** *(Raise your sword up and swing it around in the air.)*
WOMAN #2:	*(Stick your tongue out at WOMAN #1.)*
WOMAN #1:	*(Stick your tongue out at WOMAN #2.)*
SOLOMON:	**Hmm… They both claim the live baby is theirs and the dead one isn't…. Soldier?**
SOLDIER:	**Yes, your majesty?**
SOLOMON:	**Go get me a sword.**
SOLDIER:	*(Pick up the sword.)* **Here you go, your majesty.**
SOLOMON:	**That was quick.**
SOLDIER:	**Yes, of course, your majesty.**
SOLOMON:	**Alright. Take the sword and cut the baby in half. We'll give half of the baby to each woman.**
SOLDIER:	**As you wish, your majesty.** *(Take the BABY from the women.)*

NARRATOR:	**When the baby's real mother heard that, she was afraid, for her heart was full of love for her child.**
WOMAN #1:	**No! Don't do it! Give the baby to her! Let it live!**
WOMAN #2:	**Go on; cut the baby in half. That way neither of us will have a baby.**
SOLDIER:	*(Raise the sword over the BABY.)* **Should I really cut the baby in half, your majesty?**
SOLOMON:	**No! Don't hurt the baby. Give him to the first woman. She's the real mother. She wanted the baby to live no matter what. That's the kind of love a mother has.**
SOLDIER:	**Yes, your majesty.** *(Hand the BABY to WOMAN #1.)*
WOMAN #1:	*(Huge smiles, hug your BABY!)*
WOMAN #2:	*(Frown and pout.)*
NARRATOR:	**When people heard what Solomon had said and done, they were amazed! They could tell God really had given him great wisdom. And news of Solomon's decision spread throughout the land.**
EVERYONE:	*(Together)* **The end!**

(Smile, bow, and then take your seat.)

37

ELIJAH AND THE SHOWDOWN ON MT. CARMEL

BASED ON: 1 Kings 17:1, 18:1–46

BIG IDEA: On Mt. Carmel, God proved He was the one true God. Finally, the Israelites turned back to Him.

BACKGROUND: Ahab and his family were wicked rulers in the northern kingdom (Israel). As a result, God's prophet Elijah prayed that God would not send rain or dew on the land. The Israelites were worshiping Baal, a god of fertility, but one believer's prayer showed how worthless that "god" was! During the drought, God protected and provided for Elijah in miraculous ways.

Finally, after more than three years, God told Elijah to set up a showdown where He would prove once and for all that He really was the Lord.

NEW TESTAMENT CONNECTION: Elijah stood up for the Lord even when it wasn't popular and when he was in the minority. Today we are asked to do the same thing: *Therefore, since we have such a hope, we are very bold* (2 Corinthians 3:12, NIV).

CAST: You'll need 6-10 children for this skit: Narrator (girl or boy), 1-3 Baal Prophets (boys or girls), 1-3 Israelites (boys or girls), Obadiah (preferably a boy), Elijah (preferably a boy), King Ahab (preferably a boy)

PROPS: Two handfuls of raw hamburger, 12 cups of water, a bucket of water, a table, a towel to clean up with, and a blowtorch (all optional)

TOPICS: Choices, conviction, courage, faith, God's existence, God's power, ministry (of the prophets), prayer, success, worship

TIPS: Make sure you explain to all the children that the kids playing the part of the Baal Prophets aren't really praying to a false god. They're just saying their lines and pretending to be like the people long ago who didn't love the Lord. Help the audience and the readers understand that there's a difference between acting in a skit and doing something in real life.

If you use props, have the handfuls of hamburger available for the Baal Prophets and Elijah. Place the 12 cups of water on the table next to the bucket of water. When the Israelites pour water on Elijah's altar, have them pour the water on the raw hamburger. When the part comes where God's fire burns it up, pull out the blowtorch and wave it in front of the audience. (If you choose to do this, you'll need an adult to be the Narrator!)

Position the Baal Prophets next to each other on the left side of the stage, the Israelites and the Narrator next to each other on the right side of the stage, and Obadiah, Elijah, and King Ahab in the center. Bring up the stage lights, and then begin when the listeners are quiet.

Elijah and the Showdown on Mt. Carmel

DIRECTOR: Lights! Camera! Action!

NARRATOR: Long ago, God's people began worshiping made-up gods, so Elijah prayed that no rain would fall on the land.

ELIJAH: God, make the rain go away and come again some other day!

NARRATOR: During that time, the people of the land were very hot and thirsty.

ISRAELITES: *(Stick out your tongue and pant like a thirsty dog.)*

NARRATOR: Dew didn't even fall on the grass at night!

ISRAELITES: We need some dew, dudes!

NARRATOR: This went on for a long time...

ISRAELITES: *(More panting)*

NARRATOR: until finally, in the third year, God told Elijah to go to King Ahab because He was ready to send rain on the land.

ELIJAH: Whatever You say, God!

NARRATOR: Now, King Ahab had been looking for Elijah because he blamed him for the drought. He was also looking for water.

KING AHAB: Hey, Obadiah!

OBADIAH: Yes, your majesty?

KING AHAB: You're in charge of my palace, right?

OBADIAH: Of course, your majesty.

KING AHAB: Well, my royal pets are thirsty.

OBADIAH: Oh.

KING AHAB: Go through the country and look for some water to give them.

OBADIAH: Okay.

KING AHAB: Look everywhere—lakes, streams, springs, and water towers.

OBADIAH: What's a water tower?

KING AHAB: I don't know, but it sounds like it might have some water.

OBADIAH: Oh. Okay.

KING AHAB: Maybe between the two of us we'll find some water. You go that way. *(Point to the left.)*

OBADIAH: Right.

KING AHAB: No, that's left.

OBADIAH: Right.

KING AHAB: And I'll go this way. *(Point to the right.)*

OBADIAH: Right.

KING AHAB: That's right.

OBADIAH: Alright.

NARRATOR: Even though Obadiah worked for a wicked king, he loved the Lord. In fact, he had rescued 100 of God's prophets from a mean queen.

OBADIAH: I hid them in a cave! Hee, hee, hee, hee.

NARRATOR: During his trip to find water, Obadiah found something else—he found Elijah.

OBADIAH: Whoa! Is it really you?

ELIJAH: Yup, it's me. Now go back to King Ahab and tell him I wanna talk to him.

NARRATOR: So Obadiah went and set up the meeting.

KING AHAB: So, Elijah! There you are, you troublemaker!

ELIJAH: I'm not the troublemaker, you are! You and your family brought trouble on everyone because you turned away from the Lord!

NARRATOR: Ahab and his family had started worshiping made-up gods. One was called "Baal," and the other one was called "Asherah." Their idol worship caused many people to turn away from God. That made God very angry.

ELIJAH: Now call everyone in the country together at Mount Carmel. We'll have a showdown to see who the real God is!

KING AHAB: Sounds good to me.

ELIJAH:	Oh yeah, and bring all 450 prophets of Baal and 400 prophets of Asherah.
KING AHAB:	You've got a deal.
NARRATOR:	So Ahab called everyone together at Mount Carmel. Then Elijah spoke to the people of Israel.
ELIJAH:	How long are you gonna put off choosing who to serve? Huh? If the Lord is God, serve Him. If Baal is God, serve him. Quit going back and forth from one to the other!
NARRATOR:	But the people didn't say anything. They just stood there.
ISRAELITES:	Duh…
ELIJAH:	Okay. Get two bulls. We'll take turns. We'll cut 'em up and lay the meat on some wood. Then the prophets of Baal—
BAAL PROPHETS:	That's us!
ELIJAH:	Yeah, well, you can call out to your gods. I'll call on the Lord, and we'll see who sends fire. Whichever one does is the real God.
ISRAELITES:	Groovy.
NARRATOR:	So the prophets of Baal took a bull, cut it up, and laid it on the wood.
BAAL PROPHETS:	*(Together, take a handful of the raw hamburger and slap it on the table in front of you.)*
NARRATOR:	Then, all morning, they asked Baal to send fire.
BAAL PROPHETS:	*(Together, imitating cheerleaders)* Baal! Baal! Burn our meat! Send some fire! Send some heat! Burn this bull and show you're real! C'mon, Baal! Cook our meal!
NARRATOR:	But of course, no fire came because their god was just made-up.
BAAL PROPHETS:	Baal! Baal! What's the deal? Cook us up some roasted veal!
NARRATOR:	By noon, Elijah had started to make fun of them.
ELIJAH:	Yell louder! Maybe your god fell asleep! Or maybe he's going to the bathroom, or on vacation or something. Maybe he's taking a nap! Go on; see if you can wake him up.
BAAL PROPHETS:	*(Imitating cheerleaders, louder this time)* BAAL! BAAL! BURN OUR MEAT! SEND SOME FIRE! SEND SOME HEAT! BURN THIS BULL AND SHOW YOU'RE REAL! C'MON, BAAL! COOK OUR MEAL!
NARRATOR:	Then the prophets got all crazy about it. They danced around screaming and carrying on…until finally, that evening, Elijah said to the people…
ELIJAH:	Okay, everyone. It's my turn.
ISRAELITES:	Groovy.
NARRATOR:	He piled up 12 rocks, laid some wood on top, and then dug a ditch around the pile. Then he cut up the bull and laid the meat on the wood.
ELIJAH:	*(Take a handful of the raw hamburger and slap it on the table in front of you.)* **Okay. Now fill up four big jars of water and pour it on the meat.**
ISRAELITES:	Okay. *(Pour 4 cups of water on ELIJAH's hamburger.)*
ELIJAH:	Do it again.
ISRAELITES:	You asked for it! *(Pour 4 more cups of water on ELIJAH's hamburger.)*
ELIJAH:	And again.
ISRAELITES:	Whatever you say! *(Pour 4 more cups of water on ELIJAH's hamburger.)*
NARRATOR:	The wood and the meat *(and the table…)* were soaked. And water had filled the ditch around it all too.
ISRAELITES:	Groovy. Gravy.
ELIJAH:	*(Praying)* **Lord, show these people here today that this whole thing was Your idea. Prove You're real so the people will turn back to You!**
NARRATOR:	Suddenly, fire fell from heaven. *(Hold up the blowtorch, let the kids see it, then say, "Just kidding!")*

Israelites:	Whoa. Very groovy.
Narrator:	God burned up the meat, the wood, the rocks, and even the dirt and water. *(Sweep Elijah's hamburger off the table with your hand.)*
Baal Prophets:	Whoa.
Israelites:	The Lord is God! The Lord is real! So we will bow, and we will kneel! We'll worship Him and Him alone! We'll make those bad guys scream and moan!
Narrator:	Then Elijah had the false prophets rounded up...
Baal Prophets:	Uh-oh.
Narrator:	arrested...
Baal Prophets:	Yikes.
Narrator:	and killed off.
Baal Prophets:	**Ouch!** *(Stick out your tongue, tilt your head, and look dead.)*

Narrator:	Then Elijah prayed for rain, and before long, the clouds were forming, the wind was blowing, and the rain was falling at last. *(Pick up the bucket of water and splash it in the face of the Israelites.)*
Israelites:	Groovy.
Elijah:	Get out of here, King Ahab, or you're gonna get stuck in the mud!
King Ahab:	Okay, okay, I believe you now, Elijah! Whatever you say!
Narrator:	And everyone knew that the Lord is the only God. And that He really IS in control.
Everyone:	*(Together)* The end!

(Smile, bow, and then take your seat.)

JONAH AND THE BASKING SHARK

BASED ON:	Jonah 1-4
BIG IDEA:	Jonah's prejudice against the people of Nineveh caused him to resent God's compassion toward them.
BACKGROUND:	Assyria was an enemy of Israel and was famous in the ancient world for its cruelty. Nineveh was their capital city. When God called Jonah to preach repentance to the people there, Jonah wanted nothing to do with obeying God because he feared God just might turn their hearts around. Jonah didn't want the Assyrians to receive God's mercy (see Jonah 4:2). The book of Jonah ends before we find out if Jonah ever repented of his prejudice.
	God's message is for all people, and His grace is without bounds. When God wants to show compassion to someone, who are we to judge Him?
NEW TESTAMENT CONNECTION:	Jesus' story of the workers hired throughout the day to work in the vineyard (Matthew 20:1-16) and His story of the lost sons (Luke 15:11-32) have similar themes to the story of Jonah (i.e. resentment over God's grace on those we don't think are worthy of it).
	Also, Jesus referred to the story of Jonah as an illustration of His own death and resurrection (see Matthew 12:38-42).
CAST:	You'll need 4-5 children for this skit: Narrator #1 (girl or boy), Narrator #2 (girl or boy), Sailor #1 (girl or boy), Sailor #2/Jonah (preferably a boy)
PROPS:	Baseball caps and baggy jackets for the readers (optional)
TOPICS:	Basking sharks, calling, compassion, consequences, following God, God's love, God's sovereignty, grace, hiding, listening to God, ministry (of the prophets), obedience, prejudice, rebellion, second chances, stubbornness, witnessing
TIPS:	Since this script is so word-intensive and has a specific rhythm, you'll want to have the readers practice before presenting it to the other students. If you choose to present it as a rap song, give your readers colorful costumes to wear!
	To help the readers keep track of the words that are meant to rhyme with each other and the overall rhythmic patterns, rhyming words appear in all capital letters. You may wish to demonstrate how to emphasize rhyming words when reading aloud.
	Position the Narrators next to each other, and the Sailors and Jonah next to each other. (If you use four readers, have Sailor #2 also read the lines for Jonah.) Bring up the stage lights, and then begin when the listeners are quiet.

Jonah and the Basking Shark

DIRECTOR:	Lights! Camera! Action!
EVERYONE:	*(Together)* Jonah was a prophet. He was brave and TRUE; But he didn't always do what God wanted him TO.
SAILORS:	*(Together)* He tried to run away on a ship for Tar-SHISH;
NARRATORS #1 & #2	*(Together)* But the Lord sent a storm and a giant FISH...Boyz!
NARRATOR #1:	'Cause God told Jonah, "Go to NINEVEH! Tell 'em all to repent of their SINS AND THE... bad things they DO. 'Cause they haven't got a CLUE! Go, Jonah, go! I'm talking to YOU!"
EVERYONE:	*(Together)* Go, Jonah!... Go, Jonah!... Go, go, go!
NARRATOR #2:	But Jonah ran away on a ship that DAY.
NARRATOR #1:	No, he didn't...
NARRATOR #2:	No, he didn't...
NARRATOR #1:	No, he didn't OBEY.
NARRATOR #2:	Soon a storm came blowin' in over the SEA.
NARRATOR #1:	Like a hurricane—
NARRATOR #2:	Or a TSUNAMI.
NARRATOR #1:	All the sailors got scared. *(Pause)*
SAILORS:	*(Act really scared.)*
NARRATOR #2:	They were freaked and AFRAID.
SAILORS:	*(Act even more scared.)*
NARRATOR #1:	They shouted…
SAILORS:	*(Together)* Pray to your gods!
NARRATOR #1:	And they bowed, and they PRAYED.
NARRATOR #2:	But their gods didn't help 'cause their gods were PRETEND,
NARRATOR #1:	And they all thought their lives were comin' to an END.
EVERYONE:	*(Together)* We're dead!... We're dead!... We're dead, dead meat!
NARRATOR #1:	The men dumped cargo from their ship to the SEA,
NARRATOR #2:	And the captain found Jonah, on his bed ASLEEP.
EVERYONE:	*(Together)* Snore!... Snore!... Snore, snore, snore!
SAILOR #1:	Wake up! We're afraid! And we've lost our NERVE. So c'mon! Say a prayer to the God you SERVE!
NARRATOR #2:	But Jonah didn't pray 'cause he already KNEW why the Lord was mad and why the hurricane BLEW. Because...
EVERYONE:	*(Together)* Jonah was a prophet. He was brave and TRUE; But he didn't always do what God wanted him TO. He tried to run away on a ship for Tar-SHISH; But the Lord sent a storm and a giant FISH...Boyz!
SAILOR #1:	Where do you live, man? What do you DO? And why would God send a big storm to get YOU?
JONAH:	I'm runnin' AWAY. I didn't OBEY! And now I know God's not happy TODAY!
EVERYONE ELSE:	*(Together, looking at JONAH)* NO KIDDING, DUDE!
NARRATOR #2:	*(Sing to the tune of the "Gilligan's Isle" theme song.)* The weather started getting rough. The tiny ship was tossed. If not for the courage of the fearless crew—
EVERYONE ELSE:	*(Together)* Wrong!... Wrong!... Wrong, wrong song!
NARRATOR #2:	Oh.

JONAH:	It's all my fault. I disobeyed the LORD. Now save yourselves! Throw me OVERBOARD!
NARRATOR #1:	The sailors tried hard to row the boat to SHORE,
NARRATOR #2:	But the wind blew harder than it had BEFORE!
NARRATOR #1:	So they tossed our hero off into the SEA.
NARRATOR #2:	And a shark ate him up as a tasty TREAT.
NARRATOR #1:	Wait a minute! Wasn't it a whale?
NARRATOR #2:	Well, the Bible says it was a fish.
NARRATOR #1:	Yeah, so?
NARRATOR #2:	Whales are mammals, not fish. The only fish large enough to swallow a man is a shark.
NARRATOR #1:	A shark?
NARRATOR #2:	Yeah. Probably a basking shark. They have huge mouths and tiny teeth, so Jonah could easily have survived. And they grow up to 33 feet long.
NARRATOR #1:	Whoa.
EVERYONE:	*(Together)* Gulp!... Gulp!... Gulp, gulp, gulp!
NARRATOR #2:	Then the storm stopped BLOWIN'! And the waves stopped FLOWIN'!
NARRATOR #1:	So the sailors started SHOWIN' their thanks to God....
EVERYONE:	*(Together)* Pray!... Pray!... Pray, pray, pray!
NARRATOR #2:	*(After a pause)* And then...Jonah spent three days in the belly of the shark.
EVERYONE:	*(Together)* Dark!... Dark!... Dark, dark, dark!
NARRATOR #1:	Now, spending three days in the belly of a FISH
NARRATOR #2:	Is enough to make anyone do the Lord's WISH.
NARRATOR #1:	Then the fish spit him up near the Nineveh SHORE,
NARRATOR #2:	And he got another message from his mighty LORD,
NARRATOR #1:	"Jonah! Go and preach all the words I SAID! If they don't repent, then they'll all be DEAD!"
NARRATOR #2:	So Jonah walked up, smelling just like BILE
NARRATOR #1:	From the stomach
NARRATOR #2:	Of the shark
NARRATOR #1:	Where he'd been for AWHILE!
EVERYONE:	*(Together)* Yuck!... Yuck!... Yuck, yuck, yuck!
JONAH:	Forty days, that's all! Forty days, that's IT! Just forty short days is the time you GET! If you don't believe, you'll all be DEAD. So you better repent like God has SAID!
NARRATOR #2:	Well, the people heard that, and I know it's ODD,
NARRATOR #1:	But Jonah's little sermon turned 'em all to GOD.
NARRATOR #2:	They changed their minds. They changed their WAYS,
NARRATOR #1:	And they all lived past those forty DAYS.
NARRATOR #2:	They said they were sorry, and they said they were BAD.
NARRATOR #1:	And they cried, and they prayed, and they felt really SAD.
EVERYONE:	*(Together)* Waa!... Waa!... Waa, waa, waa!
NARRATOR #2:	When God saw the change, He forgave 'em ALL.
NARRATOR #1:	They believed.
NARRATOR #2:	They were saved.
NARRATOR #1:	And they had a BALL.
NARRATOR #2:	But Jonah still hadn't changed his MIND.
NARRATOR #1:	He hated those people.
NARRATOR #2:	He complained and WHINED.
NARRATOR #1:	But God asked Jonah,

44

NARRATOR #2: Why be mad at ME?
I love 'em like I loved you
in the depths of the SEA.

SAILOR #1: For our God is great.

SAILOR #2: And His love is GRAND.

SAILOR #1: And it's meant for all people
of every LAND.

SAILOR #2: So don't be whiny
and make a FUSS,

SAILOR #1: Just be thankful He gave
His love to US!

EVERYONE: *(Together)* Yeah!... Yeah!...
Yeah, yeah, yeah!

SAILOR #2: I said don't be whiny and make a—

SAILORS: *(Together)* FUSS!

SAILOR #1: Just be thankful He gave His love to—

SAILORS: *(Together)* US!

EVERYONE: *(Together)* The end!... End!...
End, end, end!

(Smile, bow, and then take your seat.)

45

FUNNY NAMES AND A FIERY FURNACE

BASED ON: Daniel 3

BIG IDEA: When King Nebuchadnezzar ordered everyone to bow and worship his golden statue, three Jewish men refused to obey. God rescued them and revealed His mighty power to the unbelieving king.

BACKGROUND: King Nebuchadnezzar was one of the most powerful rulers in the world. When he ordered everyone in the land to worship his statue, only a handful of people resisted. When they did, they were thrown into the fiery furnace, but God rescued them! They became heroes and witnesses in the land.

NEW TESTAMENT CONNECTION: The boldness and courage of these three men serve as an example for us today: *But in your hearts revere Christ as Lord. Always be prepared to give an answer to everyone who asks you to give the reason for the hope that you have. But do this with gentleness and respect* (1 Peter 3:15, NIV).

CAST: You'll need 6-8 children for this skit: Narrator (girl or boy), 1-3 Leaders (girls or boys), King Neb (preferably a boy), Shadrach (preferably a boy), Meshach (preferably a boy), Abednego (preferably a boy)

PROPS: Musical instruments, or pots and pans to bang around (optional)

TOPICS: Angels, choices, conviction, courage, faith, following God, God's power, integrity, obedience, prayer, witnessing, worship

TIPS: The Leader has a rather goofy part. Choose a child who likes to ham it up as the reader for this part. (You could use up to three people for this part.) If desired, hand out some instruments to volunteer musicians from the audience.

Make sure that whomever you choose to read the part of King Neb can actually pronounce the name "Nebuchadnezzar"!

Position Shadrach, Meshach, and Abednego next to each other on the left side of the stage, the Narrator in the center, and the Leader/s and King next to each other on the right side of the stage. Bring up the stage lights, and then begin when the listeners are quiet.

Funny Names and a Fiery Furnace

DIRECTOR:	Lights! Camera! Action!
NARRATOR:	One day, King Nebuchadnezzar set up a statue 90 feet tall.
KING NEB:	*(Excitedly)* C'mon, everybody! Come see my statue!
LEADER:	Okee-dokee, King Nudder-Butter.
KING NEB:	That's Nebuchadnezzar.
LEADER:	Oh, yeah. Right.
NARRATOR:	So all the leaders in the land gathered around the statue.
LEADER:	That's a very shiny statue, King Fuzzy-Sweater.
KING NEB:	Thank you. And it's King Nebuchadnezzar.
LEADER:	Oh, yeah. Right. Hee, hee, hee, hee.
KING NEB:	*(Proudly)* It's golden…
LEADER:	Ooh.
KING NEB:	*(Proudly)* and tall…
LEADER:	Aah.
KING NEB:	and everyone must worship the statue when the music starts.
LEADER:	Um… What happens if we don't?
KING NEB:	You'll be burned alive in a big fiery furnace.
LEADER:	Oh. I see.
NARRATOR:	Then the music started. *(If you're using musicians, they can clang their instruments at this time.)*
NARRATOR:	And the people bowed…. Well, most of the people did.
LEADER:	Um, King Never-Eat-Cheddar, three men won't bow.
KING NEB:	What? Where are they? And, um, it's King Nebuchadnezzar, by the way.
LEADER:	Oh, yeah. Right. Hee, hee, hee, hee.
KING NEB:	Bring them to me!
THREE GUYS:	*(Together)* Here we are!
KING NEB:	What are your names?
MESHACH:	Meshach.
SHADRACH:	Shadrach.
ABEDNEGO:	Abednego.
KING NEB:	Well, Mr. Flea-Shack, Backpack, and A-Funny-Bone—
MESHACH:	That's Meshach.
SHADRACH:	Shadrach.
ABEDNEGO:	And Abednego.
KING NEB:	Right. Is it true that you don't serve my gods or bow to worship my statue?
SHADRACH:	Yup.
MESHACH:	Yup.
ABEDNEGO:	Yup.
KING NEB:	Are you ready to bow and worship when the music starts?
SHADRACH:	Nope.
MESHACH:	Nope.
ABEDNEGO:	Nope.
KING NEB:	*(Angrily)* Err! Then I'll burn you alive in a big fiery furnace! And what god could save you then?
THREE GUYS:	*(Together)* O King Nebuchadnezzar—
KING NEB:	Wow, they got it right!
SHADRACH:	Our God can save us. And He WILL save us!
MESHACH:	But even if He chooses not to save us…
ABEDNEGO:	We won't EVER worship your statue.
KING NEB:	It's golden…
SHADRACH:	Yes, I see.
KING NEB:	and tall…
MESHACH:	Right.
KING NEB:	and shiny.

ABEDNEGO:	Very nice. But we're NOT gonna worship it.
KING NEB:	Err! Alright then! That's it! Tie 'em up and toss 'em in!
NARRATOR:	And so, some of the strongest soldiers in King Nob-On-His-Head-There's army—
KING NEB:	Um, that's Nebuchadnezzar's army.
NARRATOR:	Oh, yeah…right…tied up those three men and tossed 'em into the fiery furnace, which was rather like a large barbeque pit.
SHADRACH:	Whee!
MESHACH:	Whee!
ABEDNEGO:	Whee!
KING NEB:	Um, didn't we throw three men in there?
LEADER:	Yes, King Nibble-Your-Nezzar.
KING NEB:	That's King Nebuchadnezzar! Then how come I see FOUR men in there? And how come one of them looks like a god?
LEADER:	Um, I dunno….
KING NEB:	Hey, Brick-Shack, Shady-Pack, and A-Bendy-Bow, come on out!
THREE GUYS:	*(Together)* That's Meshach, Shadrach, and Abednego.
KING NEB:	Oh, yeah. Right…. Um, are you okay?
SHADRACH:	Yup.
MESHACH:	Yup.
ABEDNEGO:	Yup.
KING NEB:	You're not well done? Burned to a crisp? Or fried alive?
SHADRACH:	Nope.
MESHACH:	Nope.
ABEDNEGO:	Nope.

NARRATOR:	All the leaders gathered around them. They couldn't believe the men weren't burned, their hair wasn't singed, and their clothes didn't even smell like smoke.
LEADER:	They must have been in the nonsmoking section.
KING NEB:	Um, I don't think so…. Praise be to their God! These men would rather die than worship any other god but their own.
SHADRACH:	Yup.
MESHACH:	Yup.
ABEDNEGO:	Yup.
KING NEB:	From now on, if anyone says anything bad about their God, we'll cut him up into little tiny pieces, and then we'll bulldoze his house into the ground! Yeah, that's what we'll do!
SHADRACH:	He's rather violent, don't you think?
MESHACH:	I should say so.
ABEDNEGO:	Me too.
SHADRACH:	Yup.
MESHACH:	Yup.
ABEDNEGO:	Yup.
NARRATOR:	Then the king promoted them. And people all over the kingdom heard about the Lord because of those three brave men…
MESHACH:	Meshach.
SHADRACH:	Shadrach.
ABEDNEGO:	And Abednego.
EVERYONE:	*(Together)* The end!

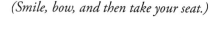

(Smile, bow, and then take your seat.)

Daniel in the Lions' Den

Based On: Daniel 6

Big Idea: God rescued Daniel from the lions' den because of his unshakable faith and life of integrity.

Background: Daniel had lived in Babylon for decades and had served as an advisor and leader under several different administrations. Through it all, he showed remarkable integrity and conviction.

In this story, when Daniel's political adversaries try to get rid of him, their plan backfires, and they end up eliminating themselves instead.

New Testament Connection: Daniel is a shining example of integrity. He didn't give in, and he didn't show off. He simply lived out his faith. We're called to do the same: *In the same way, let your light shine before others, that they may see your good deeds and glorify your Father in heaven* (Matthew 5:16, NIV).

Cast: You'll need 5 children for this skit: Narrator (girl or boy), Bad Dude #1 (girl or boy), Bad Dude #2 (girl or boy), King Darius (preferably a boy), Daniel (preferably a boy)

Props: None

Topics: Angels, conviction, following God, God's power, integrity, leadership, ministry (of the prophets), obedience, sneakiness, success, vengeance, witnessing, worship

Tips: Bad Dude #2 plays a really stupid guy. Have fun with this role!

Position the Narrator on the right side of the stage, Bad Dude #1 and Bad Dude #2 on the left side, and King Darius and Daniel in the center. Bring up the stage lights, and then begin when the listeners are quiet.

DANIEL IN THE LIONS' DEN

DIRECTOR: Lights! Camera! Action!

NARRATOR: King Darius put 120 governors over his kingdom. And he put three men in charge of them all. One of those men was named Daniel.

BAD DUDE #1: Oh! I hate Daniel!

BAD DUDE #2: *(Stupidly)* Me too.

BAD DUDE #1: I wish he were gone for good.

BAD DUDE #2: Me too.

BAD DUDE #1: Let's try to find something he's done wrong!

BAD DUDE #2: Me too!... I mean, good idea, dude!

NARRATOR: So they watched Daniel closely and checked his work, but they couldn't catch him doing anything wrong at all.

BAD DUDE #1: Ooh! I wish he'd cheat on his taxes or break the speed limit or shoplift or anything!

BAD DUDE #2: Me too. Um...what's shoplifting?

BAD DUDE #1: It's...never mind. Look, Daniel's always praying to his God, right?

BAD DUDE #2: Uh-huh.

BAD DUDE #1: Well, maybe we can use that against him.

BAD DUDE #2: Good idea, dude! Um...how are we gonna do that?

BAD DUDE #1: Don't worry.... I've got a plan.

BAD DUDE #2: Me too.

BAD DUDE #1: No, you don't!

BAD DUDE #2: Oh, yeah. Right. I forgot, dude.

NARRATOR: So the leaders who didn't like Daniel went before the king with their plan.

BAD DUDE #1: King Darius, may you live forever!

KING DARIUS: *(Happily)* Well, I hope so!

BAD DUDE #2: Live on, dude!

KING DARIUS: Thank you!

BAD DUDE #1: We have a great idea! Why don't you make a law that people have to worship you!

KING DARIUS: Hmm... Sounds good.

BAD DUDE #1: And if they don't, you'll feed 'em to some hungry lions!

KING DARIUS: Sure, why not! They won't live forever.

BAD DUDE #1: No, sir.

KING DARIUS: Well, then! Let's do it!... Um, say the thing to me again about me living forever.

BAD DUDE #1: King Darius, may you live forever!

BAD DUDE #2: Live on, dude!

KING DARIUS: Well, I hope so!

NARRATOR: Now, Daniel heard about the new law, but he didn't care. He just went on worshiping God the same as he'd always done.

BAD DUDE #1: Oh, goody! Look at that!

BAD DUDE #2: Yeah, look at that!... Um, look at what?

BAD DUDE #1: Daniel! Look at Daniel! He's praying to his God!

BAD DUDE #2: Look at that! Daniel's praying to his God! Ha, ha, ha... Um...so?

BAD DUDE #1: So we finally got him! Let's go tell the king, and he'll throw Daniel into the lions' den!

BAD DUDE #2: Me too!

BAD DUDE #1: No, not you too!

BAD DUDE #2: Oh, yeah. Right. I forgot, dude.

BAD DUDE #1: Remember that new law you made, your majesty?

KING DARIUS: Um...you didn't say the thing about me living forever.

BAD DUDE #1: *(Sighing)* Okay...King Darius, may you live forever!

BAD DUDE #2: Live on, dude!

KING DARIUS: Well, I hope so!

BAD DUDE #1: Now, remember that law?

KING DARIUS: Yes.

BAD DUDE #1: Well, Daniel broke it! He broke a rule!

BAD DUDE #2: Me too!

BAD DUDE #1: No, you didn't.

BAD DUDE #2: Oh, yeah. Right. I forgot, dude.

BAD DUDE #1: He broke your law! He prayed to his God!

KING DARIUS: Daniel prayed to his God?

BAD DUDE #1: Yeah! And now you gotta throw him into the lions' den!

KING DARIUS: Oh, no!

BAD DUDE #2: Me too.

BAD DUDE #1: Would you be quiet?

BAD DUDE #2: Okay, good idea, dude.

NARRATOR: The king tried everything he could think of to save Daniel, but it was too late. Once a law in that land was signed, it was final. It couldn't be changed.

KING DARIUS: Daniel?

DANIEL: Yes, your majesty?

KING DARIUS: May your God save you!

DANIEL: Well, I hope so.

KING DARIUS: May you live for tonight!

DANIEL: That too.

NARRATOR: They threw Daniel into the pit where the lions were and rolled a stone over the entrance. And all night long the king worried about his friend.

KING DARIUS: Oh, I can't sleep! Poor Daniel!

NARRATOR: That night the king had no food and no dancers or storytellers brought to him.

KING DARIUS: How could I eat at a time like this?

NARRATOR: Early in the morning, he hurried to the cave and had the stone rolled back.

KING DARIUS: Daniel! Was your God able to save you?

DANIEL: You better believe it! Um...I mean, yeah. King Darius, may you live forever!

KING DARIUS: Well, I hope so!

DANIEL: My God sent His angel, and He shut the lions' mouths!

KING DARIUS: Hooray!

NARRATOR: So they pulled Daniel out of the pit.

KING DARIUS: Those lions are looking pretty hungry, and I wouldn't want 'em to have to go very long without a good, healthy meal....

BAD DUDE #2: Uh-oh.

BAD DUDE #1: Um, we might be in trouble here.

KING DARIUS: Toss in those guys who were trying to get rid of Daniel!

BAD DUDE #1: I think we're dead meat....

BAD DUDE #2: Me too. Dude.

(Bad Dudes #1 and #2 step back or lie down dead on the floor.)

KING DARIUS: Yuck... *(Pause)* They didn't live forever.

DANIEL: No, they didn't, your majesty.

NARRATOR: And the king sent a decree throughout the land that everyone must respect Daniel's God.

KING DARIUS: For He's the only one who really will live forever!

DANIEL: You can say that again!

KING DARIUS: For He's the only one who really will live forever! He saves and rescues and does wonders and miracles!

DANIEL: He saved me!

NARRATOR: So after Daniel was saved, God's name was spread throughout the world.

EVERYONE: *(Together)* The end!

(Smile, bow, and then take your seat.)

Esther, the Bravest Beauty Queen

BASED ON:

Esther 1–8

BIG IDEA:

Esther's story shows us that God is faithful and works behind the scenes in everyday life to deliver and bless His people.

BACKGROUND:

King Xerxes and the Persians had conquered the Israelites and led them into captivity. In his third year of ruling from the city of Susa, King Xerxes banished his queen. After a nationwide search, he chose a Jewish girl named Esther to be the new queen. This story tells how God used her courage to protect Jews throughout the empire.

NEW TESTAMENT CONNECTION:

Esther placed her life in God's hands when she went before King Xerxes. Paul had the same kind of faith in God: *I eagerly expect and hope that I will in no way be ashamed, but will have sufficient courage so that now as always Christ will be exalted in my body, whether by life or by death* (Philippians 1:20, NIV). And we pray the same thing too.

CAST:

You'll need 5 children for this skit: Narrator (girl or boy), Haman (preferably a boy), Mordecai (preferably a boy), King Xerxes (preferably a boy), Esther (girl)

PROPS:

None

TOPICS:

Advice, bullies, choices, conviction, courage, family relationships, following God, God's sovereignty, hope, integrity, leadership, planning, prejudice, questions, resentment, success, wisdom

TIPS:

Position the Narrator on the right side of the stage, Haman and Mordecai on the left side, and King Xerxes and Esther in the center. Bring up the stage lights, and then begin when the listeners are quiet.

Esther, the Bravest Beauty Queen

DIRECTOR: Lights! Camera! Action!

NARRATOR: Long ago, there was a king named King Xerxes.

KING XERXES: Gesundheit.

NARRATOR: I wasn't sneezing. I was telling them your name.

KING XERXES: Oh, right.

NARRATOR: Well, one day he kicked his wife out of the palace because she wouldn't do what he asked her to do.

KING XERXES: Serves her right. That'll teach her a lesson!

NARRATOR: But then he got really lonely.

KING XERXES: That'll teach me a lesson! What am I gonna do?... I know! I'll search for a beautiful new queen. Why should I be lonely? After all, I am King Xerxes!

NARRATOR: Gesundheit.

KING XERXES: Thank you.

NARRATOR: So he decided to throw the first beauty pageant ever. His advisors searched throughout the land until they came to the home of a Jewish man named Mordecai…

MORDECAI: That's me!

NARRATOR: and his beautiful young cousin, Esther.

ESTHER: That's me.

MORDECAI: Esther, you know that since your parents died I've raised you as my own daughter. I've always tried to do what's best for you.

ESTHER: Yes, Mordecai. Why are you saying this? What's wrong?

MORDECAI: These men are searching for a new queen for King Xerxes.

KING XERXES: Gesundheit.

MORDECAI: Who said that?

KING XERXES: Never mind.

MORDECAI: Anyway, they may try to take you away. If they do, don't tell anyone you're a Jewish girl.

ESTHER: But why not, Mordecai?

MORDECAI: Trust me, Esther. There are people out there who don't like Jews.

ESTHER: Okay, I promise. I'll do as you say.

NARRATOR: The advisors DID notice Esther, and they DID take her back to the king. And when he saw her, his heart began to flutter.

KING XERXES: Esther wins the contest! She shall be my new queen!

NARRATOR: He placed a crown on Esther's head and threw a big party to celebrate…. Now, one of the highest officials in the government, a man named Haman, was there.

HAMAN: So the king has a new queen. I'm just glad she's not a Jew. I hate 'em all! Especially that guy Mordecai! He never bows before me.

MORDECAI: I never worship people, Haman. I'll never worship you.

NARRATOR: Then, one day Haman had an idea.

HAMAN: I know what I'll do. I'll tell the king that all Jews are bad and should be killed. Then I can get rid of Mordecai and all of his people at the same time!

NARRATOR: Well, Haman tricked the king into making a law that all the Jews should be killed. And when Mordecai found out, he was very troubled and sad.

MORDECAI: What will we do? Unless something happens, we'll all be goners!... I know, I'll send a note to Queen Esther and ask for her help.

ESTHER: Hmm… A letter from Mordecai… *(Pretend to read a letter.)* Dear Esther, we're all in danger. Perhaps you've been placed in the palace at this time to help us. Will you ask the king to save us? Love, Mordecai.

NARRATOR: Now, you remember how the king treated queens who didn't please him.

ESTHER: What shall I do?

NARRATOR: Talking to the king without being invited was dangerous. It meant death for anyone who would try it!

ESTHER: If the king isn't happy with me, he'll have me killed! But if I don't say something, my family will die. Oh, what should I do?

NARRATOR: Finally, Esther agreed to help her people. She went into the throne room and bowed low to the ground. She knew she might not walk out of there alive.

ESTHER: O King, have mercy on me!

KING XERXES: Arise, my queen! What do you want? Don't be afraid. I won't hurt you!

ESTHER: Then come to a special party. I'll ask you for a favor then.

KING XERXES: Splendid! I'll see you there, my dear!

ESTHER: And Haman is invited too.

HAMAN: Oh, goody, goody. A party!

NARRATOR: Meanwhile, Haman was preparing to have Mordecai hanged. He had a long rope brought in and ordered his helpers to build a place to hang Mordecai.

HAMAN: He'll never bother me again! *(Evil laughter.)*

NARRATOR: The first party went well. Then, a few days later Esther invited the king and Haman to a second party. It was finally time to ask for the king's help.

HAMAN: Oh, goody, goody! Another party! And by the end of the day, Mordecai will be hanged. This is gonna be a day to remember!

KING XERXES: Esther, thank you for this party. Now, I think you mentioned you have something important you want to ask me. What is it?

ESTHER: Save me, O King! Save my people and me from the man who wants to destroy us all!

KING XERXES: But who? Who would dare to harm my queen?

ESTHER: *(Point to Haman.)* He would!

KING XERXES: What?

HAMAN: Uh-oh.

ESTHER: Our enemy is Haman!

HAMAN: This might not be good.

NARRATOR: About that time one of the guards said the place to hang Mordecai was ready.

KING XERXES: What? But Mordecai is a hero! He warned me when people were planning to kill me! He saved my life! You would kill my queen and the man who saved me?

HAMAN: Uh-oh. This is not going according to plan.

KING XERXES: Guards! Take him away! You know what to do with him!

HAMAN: Um...help?

NARRATOR: That day Haman was hanged, and the king did what he could to protect the Jews from those who wanted to harm them.

KING XERXES: Mordecai!

MORDECAI: Yes, your majesty?

KING XERXES: Tell your people to protect themselves. I don't want any Jews harmed!

MORDECAI: Yes, your majesty!

KING XERXES: And it seems that with Haman's departure we have a job opening. Would you be interested in being my chief advisor?

MORDECAI: I would be honored, your majesty!

ESTHER: Oh, thank you, King Xerxes! You've saved my people.

KING XERXES: No, Esther. YOU have saved your people.

NARRATOR: And ever since that day, Jews around the world have celebrated parties of their own in honor of Esther and the time she helped rescue them from Haman's evil plan by talking to King Gesundheit—

KING XERXES: Xerxes!

NARRATOR: Oh, yeah.

EVERYONE: *(Together)* The end!

(Smile, bow, and then take your seat.)

THE BIRTH OF KING JESUS

BASED ON:	Matthew 1:18–25 and Luke 1:26–38, 2:1–7
BIG IDEA:	At precisely the right moment in history, God sent His Son, our Savior, into the world. Jesus was born in a miraculous way, just as the prophets had foretold.
BACKGROUND:	Throughout the centuries, God had promised the Jews a Savior. During the reign of King Herod, the time had come for His arrival. First, Elizabeth, the wife of a priest, was promised a special son, John the Baptist. Then her relative, Mary, received her own heavenly visitor who promised that her miraculous Son would be the Savior.
	When Jesus was born, shepherds were the first ones to hear the good news, and the first ones to share it as well.
KEY VERSE:	*But when the time had fully come God sent his Son, born of a woman, born under the law, to redeem those under the law, that we might receive adoption to sonship* (Galatians 4:4-5, NIV).
CAST:	You'll need 7-8 children for this skit: Narrator (girl or boy), Angel (girl or boy), Shepherd (girl or boy), Sheep (girl or boy), Cow (girl or boy), Mary (girl), Joseph (boy), Jesus (boy, optional)
PROPS:	A large flashlight, 1-3 pair of sunglasses, a baby doll (optional)
TOPICS:	Angels, babies, Christmas, dreams, faith, family relationships, God's love, Jesus' life, prophecy fulfillment
TIPS:	The Angel should be somewhat goofy, overly excited, and dramatic.
	If you use one pair of sunglasses, give it to Mary first. Then Joseph will use them, and finally, the Shepherd. It would probably be easier to just use three pair of sunglasses. The Angel begins with the flashlight.
	If you choose to use the doll instead of a real actor, cross off Jesus' speaking lines in the script. In that case, Mary would begin with the baby doll under her shirt or behind her.
	Position the Sheep and Cow on the left side of the stage; the Narrator and the Angel in the center; and Mary, Joseph, and Jesus on the right side of the stage. Bring up the stage lights, and then begin when the listeners are quiet.

THE BIRTH OF KING JESUS

DIRECTOR: Lights! Camera! Action!

NARRATOR: While Herod was king of the Jews, an angel appeared to a young lady named Mary.

ANGEL: *(Turn on your flashlight and shine it at MARY.)* Hello, Mary!

MARY: Hi. *(Put on the sunglasses.)* Why are you so shiny?

ANGEL: I'm an angel!

MARY: You are?

ANGEL: I am! But don't be afraid. God is with you. You are blessed!

MARY: I am?

ANGEL: You are! And you're going to have a baby.

MARY: I am?

ANGEL: You are! And your Son's name will be Jesus. He will be a king!

MARY: You don't say?

ANGEL: I do! And His kingdom will last forever!

MARY: But...I'm not even married yet.

ANGEL: God will give you this baby in a special way. Your child will be the Son of God. Nothing is impossible with God.

MARY: Cool. Then I am God's servant.

ANGEL: Yes, you are!

NARRATOR: Then the angel disappeared.

ANGEL: Bye-bye! *(Turn off the flashlight.)*

NARRATOR: Now, Mary was engaged to a man named Joseph.

JOSEPH: *(Waving)* That's me.

NARRATOR: And when he found out she was expecting a baby, he knew it wasn't his child.

JOSEPH: Uh-oh.

NARRATOR: So he thought about quietly calling off the wedding to protect Mary.

JOSEPH: If she has a baby before we get married, people will make fun of her.

NARRATOR: But that night an angel appeared to Joseph.

ANGEL: *(Turn on your flashlight and shine it at JOSEPH.)* Hello, Joseph!

JOSEPH: Hi. *(Put on the sunglasses.)* Why are you so shiny?

ANGEL: I'm an angel!

JOSEPH: You are?

ANGEL: I am! Listen, don't be scared to marry Mary!

JOSEPH: You want me to marry Mary?

ANGEL: I do! Her child is from the Holy Spirit!

JOSEPH: You don't say?

ANGEL: I do! Name the baby "Jesus"! He will save people from their sins!

JOSEPH: Okay, I will.

ANGEL: Yes, you will!

NARRATOR: Then the angel went away...

ANGEL: Bye-bye! *(Turn off the flashlight.)*

NARRATOR: and Joseph woke up.

JOSEPH: Whoa. Her baby is from God.

MARY: My baby is from God.

NARRATOR: So he stuck with Mary after all.

MARY: Thank you.

JOSEPH: You're welcome.

NARRATOR: The government wanted to start a new tax, so everyone had to go to their hometowns to be counted.

JOSEPH: This is very taxing.

MARY: No kidding.

NARRATOR: Since Joseph was from Bethlehem, he and Mary traveled there.

JOSEPH: I was born in Bethlehem!

MARY:	I have a feeling someone else is gonna be born here too.
JOSEPH:	You mean?
MARY:	Yup. The baby.
JOSEPH:	*(Nervously)* Oh, boy...
NARRATOR:	When they arrived, the hotels were already full.
JOSEPH:	It sure is crowded around here, Mary!
MARY:	I have a feeling it's gonna get even more crowded.
JOSEPH:	You mean?
MARY:	Yup. The baby.
JOSEPH:	*(More nervously)* Oh, boy...we better find a place to stay, quick!
NARRATOR:	The only place they could find was a stable.
COW:	Moo!
SHEEP:	Baa!
COW:	Moo!
SHEEP:	Baa!
JOSEPH:	Man, it sure is noisy in here!
MARY:	I have a feeling it's gonna get even more noisy.
JOSEPH:	You mean?
MARY:	Yup. The baby.
JOSEPH:	*(Really, really nervously)* Oh, boy...
COW:	Moo!
SHEEP:	Baa!
COW:	Moo!
SHEEP:	Baa!
NARRATOR:	Then the time came for the baby to be born.
JESUS:	Waa!
MARY:	Oh, Joseph! Look at my baby! *(Pull out JESUS, or the baby doll.)*
JOSEPH:	He's cute!
MARY:	He's Jesus.

JOSEPH:	*(Tickling JESUS)* Kootchie, kootchie, koo!
JESUS:	Waa!
COW:	Moo!
SHEEP:	Baa!
COW:	Moo!
SHEEP:	Baa!
JESUS:	Waa!
NARRATOR:	Nearby in the fields, shepherds were watching over their flocks.
COW:	Moo!
SHEEP:	Baa!
COW:	Moo!
SHEEP:	Baa!
NARRATOR:	*(To the COW)* Um, there weren't any cows in the field. Just sheep.
COW:	Oh. Sorry. I'll mooooooove over.
SHEEP:	Baa, baa!... Baa, baa!
NARRATOR:	And suddenly, an angel appeared to them, and God's glory shone on them!
ANGEL:	*(Turn on your flashlight and shine it at the SHEPHERD.)* Hello, shepherd!
SHEPHERD:	Hi. *(Put on the sunglasses.)* Why are you so shiny? Is that God's glory?
ANGEL:	Actually, this is a flashlight!
SHEPHERD:	Oh.
ANGEL:	You gotta use your imagination.
SHEPHERD:	I see.
ANGEL:	Yes...you do!
NARRATOR:	The shepherds were scared.... Um, look scared.
SHEPHERD:	*(Act terrified.)*
NARRATOR:	But the angel said...
ANGEL:	Don't be scared! It's only a flashlight!
NARRATOR:	No, no, no. The angel said...
ANGEL:	Don't be scared! I have good news that will bring joy to everyone!
SHEPHERD:	You do?

ANGEL:	I DO! Tonight the Savior, Christ the Lord, was born in Bethlehem!
SHEPHERD:	He was?
ANGEL:	HE WAS! You'll find Him lying in a manger, wrapped in blankets!
SHEPHERD:	I will?
ANGEL:	YOU WILL!
NARRATOR:	Suddenly, a whole crowd of angels appeared in the sky, praising God—
ANGEL:	—And waving flashlights. *(Wave your flashlight.)*
NARRATOR:	No! Saying...
ANGEL:	Glory to God on high! And peace on earth to all His people!
NARRATOR:	Then the angels were gone.
ANGEL:	Bye-bye! *(Turn off the flashlight.)*
NARRATOR:	And the shepherds went to the stable and found Mary...
MARY:	I just had a baby!
NARRATOR:	and Joseph...
JOSEPH:	She just had a baby!
NARRATOR:	and Jesus...

JESUS:	Waa! Waa! Waa!
NARRATOR:	and the animals.
COW:	Moo!
SHEEP:	Baa!
COW:	Moo!
SHEEP:	Baa!
NARRATOR:	And when the shepherds left, they told everyone the story.
SHEPHERD:	You're not gonna believe this, but it's totally true!
COW & SHEEP:	It is?
ANGEL:	IT IS! *(Turn on your flashlight and wave it around.)*
COW:	Moo!
SHEEP:	Baa!
COW:	Moo!
SHEEP:	Baa!
NARRATOR:	And all who heard their story were impressed and amazed!
EVERYONE:	*(Together)* The end!

(Smile, bow, and then take your seat.)

The Arrival of the Wise Men

Based On:	Matthew 2:1–12
Big Idea:	Jesus truly is a Savior for all nations. After His birth, Gentile astronomers were more interested in finding and worshiping Him than the Jewish religious leaders in Jerusalem were.
Background:	After Jesus was born in the stable, a star appeared and a group of Magi (i.e. wise men or astronomers) from the East sought out the baby to worship Him. Many Bible scholars believe that Balaam's prophecy in Numbers 24:17 was the prophecy that led the Magi to seek Christ when the star appeared (see Matthew 2:2). Even though the religious scholars of that time knew about the coming Messiah, they showed no real interest in going to meet Him for themselves.
Key Verse:	*On coming to the house, they saw the child with his mother Mary, and they bowed down and worshiped him. Then they opened their treasures and presented him with gifts of gold, frankincense and myrrh* (Matthew 2:11, NIV).
Cast:	You'll need 5-7 children for this skit. If you only have five students, one person could read all of the Wise Guys' parts. Preferably, assign the lines to three readers: Narrator (girl or boy), 3 Wise Guys (boys or girls), Scholar (boy or girl), King Herod (preferably a boy), Mary (girl)
Props:	None
Topics:	Astronomical anomalies, Christmas, following God, God's promises, jealousy, Jesus' life, listening to God, wisdom, worship
Tips:	Position the Wise Guys and Mary on the left side of the stage, King Herod and the Narrator in the center, and the Scholar on the right side of the stage. Bring up the stage lights, and then begin when the listeners are quiet.

THE ARRIVAL OF THE WISE MEN

DIRECTOR: Lights! Camera! Action!

NARRATOR: After Jesus was born, His parents moved into a house in Bethlehem.

MARY: Good thing. That stable was stinky! *(Wave your hand in front of your face.)* Whew, baby!

NARRATOR: One day some wise men arrived from the East.

WISE GUY #1: We are wise!

WISE GUY #2: We are guys!

WISE GUY #3: We're a bunch of wise guys!

NARRATOR: And they went to the city of Jerusalem to speak with King Herod.

WISE GUY #1: Hello, Harry.

KING HEROD: That's King Herod.

WISE GUY #1: Oh. Hi, King Harry Head.

KING HEROD: I'm not King Harry Head!

WISE GUY #3: Oh. Are you bald?

KING HEROD: *(Sighing)* What do you want?

WISE GUY #2: Where's the baby who has been born King of the Jews?

KING HEROD: Baby? You're looking for a BABY who is a KING?

WISE GUYS: *(Together)* Yup!

KING HEROD: A BABY KING?

WISE GUYS: *(Together)* Yup!

KING HEROD: What are you—a bunch of wise guys?

WISE GUYS: *(Together)* Yup!

WISE GUY #1: We are wise!

WISE GUY #2: We are guys!

WISE GUY #3: We're a bunch of wise guys!

KING HEROD: Oh.

WISE GUY #3: We saw His star glowing in the sky and have come to worship Him.

KING HEROD: WORSHIP Him?

WISE GUYS: *(Together)* Yup!

NARRATOR: Well, as you can imagine, King Herod was not too happy to hear about that.

KING HEROD: I'm not too happy to hear about that.

NARRATOR: After all, HE was the king, and he didn't want any Jewish babies taking over his kingdom. So he called for his Bible teachers.

SCHOLAR: Yes, your majesty?

KING HEROD: There are a bunch of wise guys here—

WISE GUY #1: *(Quickly)* We are wise!

WISE GUY #2: We are guys!

WISE GUY #3: We're a bunch of wise guys!

KING HEROD: —who say that a new king is born. So where's the Christ supposed to be born?

SCHOLAR: Well, that's easy—in Bethlehem. Just like the prophets said.

KING HEROD: Bethlehem, huh?

SCHOLAR: Yup.

KING HEROD: Okay, then.

SCHOLAR: Anything else?

KING HEROD: No. Now get outta here.

SCHOLAR: Okay. Don't get feisty King Harry Head.

KING HEROD: That's Herod! KING Herod!

NARRATOR: Then King Herod called a secret meeting with the wise men.

WISE GUY #1: We are wise!

WISE GUY #2: We are guys!

WISE GUY #3: We're a bunch of wise guys!

KING HEROD: Yes, yes, I know.... Listen, when did that star first appear?

WISE GUY #1: Well...it was a while ago....

WISE GUY #2: I'd say almost two years ago....

WISE GUY #3:	It's been a long trip.
KING HEROD:	Okay, I see.... Well, go and worship the baby. He's in Bethlehem.
WISE GUY #1:	He is? Cool!
KING HEROD:	When you find Him, come back and let me know so I can kill—I mean COME and worship Him too.
WISE GUY #2:	*(Suspiciously)* Right...
NARRATOR:	So they left the king, and the star appeared to them again.
WISE GUY #3:	Star light! Star bright! I see that star again tonight!
NARRATOR:	And it led them to the place where Jesus was.
WISE GUY #1:	That's one smart star!
WISE GUY #2:	I'll say!
NARRATOR:	In the house, they found Mary…
MARY:	Hi, there.
NARRATOR:	and Jesus.
WISE GUY #3:	Your Majesty!
NARRATOR:	They bowed low and worshiped Him.
WISE GUYS:	*(Together, bowing)* JESUS IS THE KING OF ALL! JESUS IS THE KING OF ALL!
NARRATOR:	They opened up treasure chests and gave Him and His mother gold…
MARY:	Why, thank you!
NARRATOR:	incense…
MARY:	You're too kind!

NARRATOR:	and myrrh.
MARY:	Myrrh? What's myrrh?
WISE GUY #1:	It's a fragrant gum resin that's extracted from a variety of vegetative life forms in Arabia and East Africa.
WISE GUY #2:	It's often used in the production of incense, perfumes...
WISE GUY #3:	And various types of colognes.
MARY:	How do you know that?
WISE GUY #1:	We are wise!
WISE GUY #2:	We are guys!
WISE GUY #3:	We're a bunch of wise guys!
MARY:	Oh. I see.
NARRATOR:	Then they left by another route because God had warned them not to return to King Harry Head—
KING HEROD:	That's Herod! KING Herod! I am KING HEROD!
NARRATOR:	Like I said, King Harry Head, because he wanted to hurt Jesus. But those wise men listened to God…and do you know why they listened to God?
MARY:	They were wise!
SCHOLAR:	They were guys!
KING HEROD:	They're a bunch of wise guys!
WISE GUYS:	*(Together)* Yup!
EVERYONE:	*(Together)* The end!

(Smile, bow, and then take your seat.)

THE FIRST PALM SUNDAY

BASED ON: Matthew 21:1–11, Mark 11:1–11, Luke 19:28–44, and John 12:12–19

BIG IDEA: Jesus arrived in Jerusalem to an outpouring of public support. The people recognized Him as the long-awaited deliverer of the Jews. Yet, knowing their hearts, Jesus couldn't share in their joy.

BACKGROUND: The crowds in Jerusalem had heard about Jesus raising Lazarus from the dead and about the other wonderful miracles He'd done. So, when Jesus arrived at the beginning of the Passover celebration, the people recognized Him as a king in David's lineage, and they rushed to meet Him.

The Jews were looking for an earthly king and deliverer, but Jesus had a different type of kingdom to establish (see John 18:36). He even burst into tears as He thought of Jerusalem's spiritual rejection of God (see Luke 19:41-44).

(Note: Matthew mentions that both a donkey and a colt were present at Jesus' procession on Palm Sunday; the other Gospel accounts only mention one or the other.)

KEY VERSE: *The crowds that went ahead of him and those that followed shouted,*
> *"Hosanna to the Son of David!"*
> *"Blessed is he who comes in the name of the Lord!"*
> *"Hosanna in the highest heaven!"* (Matthew 21:9, NIV).

CAST: You'll need 7-10 children for this skit: Narrator (girl or boy), Donkey (girl), Baby Donkey (girl or boy), 1-2 Disciples (boys or girls), 2-4 Crowd (boys or girls), Jesus (boy)

PROPS: A CD of rock music and a boom box (optional)

TOPICS: Holy Week, Jesus' life, Palm Sunday, prophecy fulfillment, worship

TIPS: If you use more than one person to play the part of the Disciples, they should say all of their lines together as a group. Cue the CD so you can play 10-15 seconds of a rock song during the presentation.

Position the Donkey and the Baby Donkey on the left side of the stage, the Narrator and the Crowd in the center, and the Disciples and Jesus on the right side of the stage. Bring up the stage lights, and then begin when the listeners are quiet.

The First Palm Sunday

DIRECTOR: Lights! Camera! Action!

NARRATOR: One day Jesus and His friends were walking toward Jerusalem.

JESUS: C'mon, everybody! We're almost there!

NARRATOR: As they came closer to the city, He sent two of them ahead to get a donkey.

DONKEY: Hee-haw.

JESUS: Go to the village up ahead. I need you to get Me something....

DISCIPLES: Okee-dokee!

JESUS: No, not a dokee, a donkey.

DISCIPLES: Oh...okee-donkey!

JESUS: Right. You'll find a donkey…

DONKEY: Hee-haw.

JESUS: and her baby.

BABY DONKEY: Hee-haw. Goo, goo.... Hee-haw. Gaa, gaa.

JESUS: Untie them and bring them here.

DISCIPLES: Okee-dokee...donkey, donkey!

JESUS: Right. And if anyone asks you about it, just tell 'em I sent you. I'll send back the donkeys when I'm done.

DISCIPLES: Okee-dokee!

NARRATOR: So the disciples went and found the donkey.

DONKEY: Hee-haw.

DISCIPLES: Hello, Mr. Donkey.

DONKEY: That's Mrs. Donkey.

DISCIPLES: Oh, sorry.

DONKEY: Hee-haw.

NARRATOR: They also found the baby donkey.

DISCIPLES: Hello, Baby Donkey.

BABY DONKEY: Hee-haw. Goo, goo.... Hee-haw. Gaa, gaa.

DISCIPLES: Okee-dokee, donkeys. Let's go!

NARRATOR: The disciples brought the donkey and the colt back to Jesus.

DISCIPLES: Here You go!

NARRATOR: Jesus sat on the baby donkey.

BABY DONKEY: Ouch.

JESUS: Sorry about that.

BABY DONKEY: Hee-haw.

NARRATOR: Some people cut down branches.

CROWD: *(Together)* Timber!

NARRATOR: Just the branches, not the whole tree.

CROWD: *(Together)* Oh...sawdust!

NARRATOR: And they put the branches on the road while other people put their coats on the road—

CROWD: *(Together)* We coated the road!

NARRATOR: That's right...and they all shouted…

CROWD: *(Together)* Our Savior is here!
Our Savior is near!
From the family of David,
it's finally clear!
Hosanna! Hosanna! Hosanna!
Let's sing!
In the name of the Lord,
He is blessed! He is King!

NARRATOR: Everyone else was asking each other, "Who is this guy?"

DISCIPLES: *(Together)* It's Jesus!

CROWD: *(Together)* Oh. Cool....
Our Savior is here!
Our Savior is near!
From the family of David,
it's finally clear!
Hosanna! Hosanna! Hosanna!
Let's sing!
In the name of the Lord,
He is blessed! He is King!

NARRATOR: But the religious leaders were upset and told Jesus to make them stop saying those things.

JESUS: But if the people are quiet, the stones will start singing!

63

NARRATOR: Jesus said that because nature is made to praise God. If we don't do it, the rocks will burst into song!

DISCIPLES: It'd turn into a rock song!

NARRATOR: Right!

CROWD: *(Loudly, together)* Our Savior is here!
Our Savior is near!
From the family of David,
it's finally clear!
Hosanna! Hosanna! Hosanna!
Let's sing!
A ROCK SONG TO GOD—
TO JESUS OUR KING!

(Turn your script into an air guitar, and then jump and jam for a little while.)

DIRECTOR: *(Turn on the CD and play 10-15 seconds of rock music.)*

NARRATOR: And yet, despite all the joy, Jesus was sad and cried as He came into the city.

JESUS: Oh, Jerusalem! If only you knew the way of peace!

NARRATOR: The people there had turned away from God many times.

JESUS: One day soon, your enemies will knock you down....

NARRATOR: *(After a pause)* And so, the people welcomed Jesus into their town.

CROWD: *(Together)* Our Savior is here!

NARRATOR: But some failed to welcome Him into their hearts.

JESUS: And that's why I cried.

NARRATOR: Then, when Jesus was done riding into town, He sent the donkey...

DONKEY: Hee-haw.

NARRATOR: and the baby donkey...

BABY DONKEY: Hee-haw. Goo, goo....
Hee-haw. Gaa, gaa.

NARRATOR: back to their owners.

DISCIPLES: Okee-dokee, donkey, donkeys!...
Let's go!

NARRATOR: And ever since then, Christians all over the world have celebrated that day when Jesus rode into town…

DISCIPLES: *(Together)* We call it Palm Sunday!

NARRATOR: because that's the day the people waved palm branches and shouted…

CROWD: *(Together)* Our Savior is here!
Our Savior is near!
From the family of David,
it's finally clear!
Hosanna! Hosanna! Hosanna!
Let's sing!
In the name of the Lord,
He is blessed! He is King!

EVERYONE: *(Together)* The end!

(Smile, bow, and then take your seat.)

THE DEATH OF JESUS

BASED ON: Matthew 27:11–54, Mark 15:1–5, Luke 23:1–25, and John 18:28–40

BIG IDEA: Jesus died on the cross to provide a way for sinners to be saved.

BACKGROUND: After Jesus was betrayed by Judas, He was falsely accused of blasphemy and political dissension. Finally, He was condemned to die.

An earthquake and many other miraculous signs accompanied the death of Jesus, including dead believers being raised to life (see Matthew 27:51-53)! But the greatest miracle occurs for those who believe in Him as their Savior. For them, death is simply the doorway to heaven.

KEY VERSE: *For Christ also suffered once for sins, the righteous for the unrighteous, to bring you to God. He was put to death in the body but made alive in the Spirit* (1 Peter 3:18, NIV).

CAST: You'll need 5 children for this skit: 3 Storytellers (girls or boys), Pilate (boy), Jesus (boy)

PROPS: None

TOPICS: Choices, conviction, death, faith, grief and loss, Holy Week, Jesus' life, loneliness, prophecy fulfillment, purpose, suffering

TIPS: *This is the most serious drama in the whole book. There aren't any humorous lines or any jokes in the script.*

In this retelling of the death of Christ, be aware of the lighting. You may wish to turn the lights low, or lower them during the drama. If you have red filters for the lights, use those. Consider positioning your readers scattered across the stage rather than in a straight line.

Be aware that this drama ends with Jesus' death. It doesn't have a happy ending. As you teach this lesson, end by pointing to the hope of Easter and the risen Christ.

Position the Storytellers next to each other in the center of the stage with Pilate and Jesus to each side of them. Bring up the stage lights, and then begin when the listeners are quiet.

For this drama, rather than saying, "Lights! Camera! Action!" to begin, just nod to the actors when you're ready to start.

THE DEATH OF JESUS

TELLER #1: During the Jewish Passover festival,

TELLER #2: Jesus was led to the high priest's home.

TELLER #3: Very early in the morning,

TELLER #2: The high council met to discuss their next step.

TELLER #3: They tied up Jesus,

TELLER #1: And took Him to Pilate, the Roman governor.

TELLER #2: Meanwhile, the leading priests stirred up the mob.

TELLER #1: "Crucify Him!" they shouted. "Crucify Him!"

TELLER #2: So Pilate, hoping to please the crowd,

TELLER #3: Ordered that Jesus be whipped,

TELLER #2: And then turned Him over to the Roman soldiers,

TELLER #1: To crucify Him.

TELLER #3: To crucify Him.

TELLER #2: To crucify Him.

PILATE: Which of the two do you want me to release to you?

TELLERS #2 & #3: *(Together)* Barabbas!

PILATE: What shall I do, then, with Jesus who is called Christ?

TELLERS #2 & #3: *(Together)* Crucify Him!

PILATE: Why? What crime has He committed?

TELLERS #2 & #3: *(Together, louder)* Crucify Him!

TELLER #1: When Pilate saw that a riot was starting, he washed his hands in front of the crowd.

PILATE: I'm innocent of this man's blood!

TELLERS #2 & #3: *(Together)* His death is our fault, not yours!

TELLER #1: They led Jesus out of the city to a hill called "The Place of the Skull."

TELLER #2: And there they crucified Him.

TELLER #3: They crucified two robbers with Him, one at His right and the other at His left with Jesus in the middle. It was nine in the morning when they crucified Him.

JESUS: Father, forgive them, for they do not know what they are doing.

TELLER #2: Above His head they put a sign: THIS IS JESUS, THE KING OF THE JEWS.

TELLER #3: Those who passed by made fun of Jesus, shaking their heads and saying, "If You're such a great Savior, save Yourself! Come down from the cross, if You really are the Son of God!"

TELLER #1: One of the robbers who hung there insulted Him as well. "Hey, aren't You supposed to be the Savior? Then save Yourself and save us, too!"

TELLER #3: But the other guy scolded him.

TELLER #2: Aren't you afraid of God? We're getting what we deserve. But He hasn't done anything wrong.... Jesus, remember me when You enter Your kingdom.

JESUS: I tell you the truth, today you'll be with Me in heaven.

TELLER #3: From noon until three o'clock, darkness came over the land because the Light of the world was dying.

JESUS: My God, My God, why have You left Me alone?

TELLER #1: And when Jesus had cried out again in a loud voice, He gave up His spirit.

JESUS: It is finished.

TELLER #2: *(After a pause)* The Light of the world...

TELLER #3: The Savior of all...

TELLER #1: The King of the Jews...

TELLER #2: Jesus, Himself, had died.

TELLER #3: A Roman soldier who was watching everything was so impressed that he praised God and said, "Surely this man was the Son of God."

TELLER #1: When the people saw what took place, they lowered their heads sadly and walked away.

(Lower your head and silently take your seat.)

Jesus Is Alive!

Based On: Matthew 27:5—28:10, Mark 15:40—16:11, Luke 24:1–12, and John 20:1–18

Big Idea: On Easter morning, Jesus rose from the dead to rescue sinners everywhere. He appeared first to Mary Magdalene.

Background: After Jesus rose from the dead, He appeared first to His friend Mary Magdalene (sometimes referred to as Mary of Magdala, since that's the town she was from), a woman out of whom He had cast seven demons.

At first she was sad when she couldn't find His body. She thought someone had taken it away, but she soon believed in His resurrection. She spread the news and let others know that Jesus truly was alive again!

Key Verse: *Mary Magdalene went to the disciples with the news: "I have seen the Lord!"* (John 20:18, NIV).

Cast: You'll need 4 children for this skit. Be aware that Narrator #1 also plays the part of Mary Magdalene, and Narrator #3 also plays the part of Jesus and Peter: Narrator #1 (preferably a girl), Narrator #2 (girl or boy), Narrator #3 (preferably a boy), Sign Holder (girl or boy)

Props: Two signs. One that reads, "Sadly..." another that reads, "Excitedly!" (optional)

Topics: Angels, doubt, Easter, faith, forgiveness, God's love, God's sovereignty, Holy Week, hope, Jesus' life, new life, Peter, prophecy fulfillment, questions, second chances

Tips: Teach the audience the chorus. Encourage the children to ask the person next to them, "Have you heard?" and then turn to the person on the other side and ask again, "Have you heard?" and then turn back to the first person and ask, "Have you heard the news about Jesus?" Repeat the whole refrain process again to complete the chorus. Explain that sometimes they will say it sadly...and sometimes excitedly!

The Sign Holder is responsible for holding up the appropriate sign. (If you have younger children, you may wish to draw a frowny face for the sad sign, and a smiley face for the excited sign).

Position the Narrators on stage as desired. The Sign Holder can stand off to either side of them. Bring up the stage lights, and then begin when the listeners are quiet.

JESUS IS ALIVE!

DIRECTOR:	Lights! Camera! Action!
NARRATOR #1:	Mary Magdalene was a friend of Jesus.
NARRATOR #2:	She'd been friends with Jesus ever since He made seven demons leave her alone.
NARRATOR #3:	But now she was sad.
NARRATOR #2:	She had seen Him on the cross.
NARRATOR #1:	And she had watched Him die.
SIGN HOLDER:	*(Hold up the SAD sign.)*
AUDIENCE & ACTORS:	*(Together, sadly)* **Have you heard?... Have you heard?... Have you heard the news about Jesus?...***(Repeat)*
SIGN HOLDER:	*(Put down the sign.)*
NARRATOR #1:	Jesus was the one she had followed.
NARRATOR #2:	Jesus was the one she had listened to.
NARRATOR #3:	Jesus was the one she had loved.
NARRATOR #1:	Jesus was the one she had told everyone about!
NARRATOR #2:	She had always been excited about that!
SIGN HOLDER:	*(Hold up the EXCITED sign.)*
AUDIENCE & ACTORS:	*(Together, excitedly)* **Have you heard?... Have you heard?... Have you heard the news about Jesus?...** *(Repeat)*
SIGN HOLDER:	*(Put down the sign.)*
NARRATOR #1:	But then the soldiers arrested Him!
NARRATOR #2:	They led Him up the hill!
NARRATOR #3:	They nailed Him to the cross!
NARRATOR #1:	And then...Jesus had died.
NARRATOR #2:	Mary had hoped He would be the one to rescue her people.
NARRATOR #3:	Mary had hoped He would be her Savior.
NARRATOR #1:	But now her hope was gone.
SIGN HOLDER:	*(Hold up the SAD sign.)*
AUDIENCE & ACTORS:	*(Together, sadly)* **Have you heard?... Have you heard?... Have you heard the news about Jesus?***(Repeat)*
SIGN HOLDER:	*(Put down the sign.)*
NARRATOR #3:	That was three days ago.
NARRATOR #2:	She'd watched where they buried Him. She saw it all.
NARRATOR #1:	She saw the tomb. She saw them put a stone in front of the opening.
NARRATOR #2:	And now it was Sunday, early in the morning.
NARRATOR #3:	Just as the sun was coming up, she went with some other women to find His body....
NARRATOR #2:	To put spices on His body.
NARRATOR #1:	But she wondered how they could ever roll that big stone away.
SIGN HOLDER:	*(Hold up the SAD sign.)*
AUDIENCE & ACTORS:	*(Together, sadly)* **Have you heard?... Have you heard?... Have you heard the news about Jesus?** *(Repeat)*
SIGN HOLDER:	*(Put down the sign.)*
NARRATOR #1:	And now there is the tomb....
NARRATOR #2:	But where is the stone?
NARRATOR #3:	And who are those men in white?
NARRATOR #2:	Angels!
NARRATOR #1:	Are they angels?
NARRATOR #3:	Could they really be angels!
SIGN HOLDER:	*(Hold up the EXCITED sign.)*
AUDIENCE & ACTORS:	*(Together, excitedly)* **Have you heard?... Have you heard?... Have you heard the news about Jesus?...** *(Repeat)*
SIGN HOLDER:	*(Put down the sign.)*
NARRATOR #2:	Then, an angel said...
NARRATOR #1:	Jesus isn't here! He's alive! He's alive!
NARRATOR #3:	Alive? He's alive? Could it even be true?

Narrator #2:	Mary ran down the road.
Narrator #1:	She ran back to town.
Narrator #2:	She ran to the home of Peter and John.
Narrator #3:	*(As Peter)* What is it, Mary? What's wrong?
Sign Holder:	*(Hold up the EXCITED sign.)*
Audience & Actors:	*(Together, excitedly)* Have you heard?... Have you heard?... Have you heard the news about Jesus?... *(Repeat)*
Sign Holder:	*(Put down the sign.)*
Narrator #1:	He's gone! He's missing! Oh, where could He be?
Narrator #2:	So they ran to the tomb to see for themselves.
Narrator #3:	And they found it all just like she said.
Narrator #1:	Peter didn't know what to think, but John believed.
Sign Holder:	*(Hold up the EXCITED sign.)*
Audience & Actors:	*(Together, excitedly)* Have you heard?... Have you heard?... Have you heard the news about Jesus?...*(Repeat)*
Sign Holder:	*(Put down the sign.)*
Narrator #1:	When Mary got back to the tomb, she saw the angel.
Narrator #2:	"Why are you sad?" asked the angel.
Narrator #3:	"Why are you sad?" asked a man nearby.
Narrator #1:	"They've taken my Lord," she said. "And I don't know where they've put Him!"
Narrator #3:	"Mary, it's Me!" said the man by the tomb. "It's Me! It's Me! It's ME!"

Narrator #1:	Teacher? Teacher!
Narrator #3:	Tell My friends I'll see them soon. Tell them I've gone to see My Father and your Father...My God and your God! Go and tell them! Tell them all!
Narrator #2:	So that's just what she did....
Sign Holder:	*(Hold up the EXCITED sign.)*
Audience & Actors:	*(Together, VERY excitedly)* Have you heard?... Have you heard?... Have you heard the news about Jesus?... *(Repeat)*
Sign Holder:	*(Put down the sign.)*
Narrator #1:	And the news spread throughout the land...
Narrator #2:	And through the years...
Narrator #3:	And now it has reached us here today!
Narrator #2:	Jesus isn't dead. He's alive! He's alive!
Narrator #1:	And He wants everyone everywhere to hear...
Narrator #3:	And believe...
Narrator #2:	And share the news with others!
Sign Holder:	*(Hold up the EXCITED sign.)*
Audience & Actors:	*(Together, SUPER excitedly)* **HAVE YOU HEARD?... HAVE YOU HEARD?... HAVE YOU HEARD THE NEWS ABOUT JESUS?...***(Repeat)*
Sign Holder:	*(Put down the sign.)*
Everyone:	*(Together)* **JESUS IS ALIVE! The end!**

(Smile, bow, and then take your seat.)

THE ROAD TO EMMAUS

BASED ON: Luke 24:13–43

BIG IDEA: Jesus appeared to two of His followers on the road to Emmaus. He revealed His identity to them and shared how the Old Testament had been pointing all along to the events of the last couple of days.

BACKGROUND: After Jesus arose from the dead, His Jewish disciples had a tough time reconciling all the events of the previous couple of days with their preconceptions of the Messiah. They thought their Savior would deliver them in a physical sense from bondage and political oppression. They didn't realize He would deliver them in a much deeper, spiritual sense from sin itself.

On the afternoon of the first Easter, two of Jesus' followers were on their way from Jerusalem to a neighboring village. Jesus appeared to them and, after they explained to Him their disappointment and confusion, He retold the Old Testament story to them, showing how it all pointed to Him.

After they realized who He was, they rushed all the way back to Jerusalem and shared the news: "Jesus really is alive!"

Some Bible scholars believe this couple was Cleopas and his wife, Mary (see John 19:25). This script is written from that perspective.

KEY VERSE: *They asked each other, "Were not our hearts burning within us while he talked with us on the road and opened the Scriptures to us?"* (Luke 24:32, NIV).

CAST: You'll need 4-5 children for this skit. If you only have four students, one person could read all of the Narrators' parts: Narrator #1 (girl or boy), Narrator #2 (girl or boy), Cleopas (preferably a boy), Mary (preferably a girl), Jesus (boy)

PROPS: None

TOPICS: Disappointment, Easter, faith, ghosts, God's promises, God's Word, grief and loss, Holy Week, hope, Jesus' life, prophecy fulfillment, questions

TIPS: Position the Narrator/s and Jesus next to each other on stage, and Cleopas and Mary next to each other. Bring up the stage lights, and then begin when the listeners are quiet.

THE ROAD TO EMMAUS

DIRECTOR: Lights! Camera! Action!

NARRATOR #1: On the afternoon of the first Easter…

NARRATOR #2: Two of Jesus' friends were walking from Jerusalem to a town called Emmaus, about 7 miles away.

MARY: Whew. That's a long walk.

CLEOPAS: No kidding.

NARRATOR #1: And as they walked, they talked about everything that had just happened.

CLEOPAS: I don't get it. I really thought He would be the one. The Savior.

MARY: Yeah, me too.

CLEOPAS: And now people say He's alive!

MARY: It's weird, isn't it?

CLEOPAS: Yeah. I'll say.

NARRATOR #2: Suddenly, Jesus appeared.

NARRATOR #1: He caught up with them on the road, but they didn't know who He was.

JESUS: Hey, how's it going?

CLEOPAS: *(Angrily)* How do you think?

JESUS: What do you mean?

CLEOPAS: Don't you know about all the things that have been going on?

JESUS: What things?

CLEOPAS: The things about Jesus from Nazareth!

MARY: Yeah, He was a prophet.

CLEOPAS: He did miracles!

JESUS: Really?

CLEOPAS: Yes! Everyone knew He came from God, but our leaders had Him killed.

MARY: We were hoping He would be the one to free Israel!

JESUS: Oh.

CLEOPAS: Anyway, that was three days ago.

MARY: And now, this morning some women surprised us.

CLEOPAS: They said they went to the tomb, and His body was gone.

JESUS: Gone? Where was it?

CLEOPAS: That's the thing—no one knows!

JESUS: Wow.

MARY: Then they saw some angels.

JESUS: Angels!

MARY: Yeah! And the angels said He was alive!

JESUS: Really.

CLEOPAS: Yup. Some of our friends went to check it out, and it's true! He's not there!

JESUS: How about that.

CLEOPAS: But…

JESUS: But what?

CLEOPAS: But it's just too hard to believe He could really be alive again.

MARY: We were really hoping He would be the one.

NARRATOR #1: Now, those two weren't exactly the brightest streetlamps on the block, if you know what I mean….

JESUS: *(Sighing)* You are so slow to believe!

CLEOPAS: Huh?

MARY: What are you talking about?

JESUS: Don't play stupid with Me!

CLEOPAS: We're not playing!

JESUS: I was afraid of that…. Look, how come you don't believe the prophets?

CLEOPAS: Huh?

MARY: What do you mean?

NARRATOR #1: Folks, the wheel was spinning, but the hamster was dead….

JESUS:	Didn't they write long ago that the Savior would need to suffer all these things and then die?
MARY:	Um...I don't know.
CLEOPAS:	Did they?
NARRATOR #1:	They were a few clowns short of a circus....
JESUS:	*(Sighing again)* Okay, listen carefully.
NARRATOR #2:	Then, beginning with Moses and the prophets, Jesus explained the Bible to them.
NARRATOR #1:	He showed them it was all coming true.
NARRATOR #2:	And He showed them it was all about Him!
NARRATOR #1:	Then they arrived at the town.
JESUS:	Listen, I'm going on a little farther—
CLEOPAS:	No, stay here with us!
MARY:	Yeah, it's almost suppertime. Please! Pretty please with sugar on top?
JESUS:	Oh...okay.
NARRATOR #2:	So they all sat down for supper, and Jesus said a prayer…
NARRATOR #1:	And then He took the bread and broke it.
CLEOPAS:	Hey, you do that just like this guy we used to know...
MARY & CLEOPAS:	*(Together)* JESUS!
NARRATOR #2:	And then Jesus disappeared.
CLEOPAS:	Where did He go?
MARY:	I don't know!
CLEOPAS:	It was Him, right?
MARY:	Yeah! It was Him all along!
CLEOPAS:	Oh, I can't believe we didn't notice it earlier!
NARRATOR #1:	The gas was in the tank, but the spark plugs just weren't firing....
MARY:	Hmm... When He was telling us all those things, didn't you feel God's power in your heart?

CLEOPAS:	Yes, I did!
NARRATOR #2:	Then they hurried all the way back to Jerusalem that night.
CLEOPAS:	Whew. We should have taken the bus!
MARY:	There aren't any buses!
CLEOPAS:	Why not?
MARY:	They won't be invented for, like, 2000 years!
CLEOPAS:	That's a long time to wait for a bus.
NARRATOR #1:	They found the other disciples and told them all about meeting Jesus on the road.
MARY:	It was Jesus the whole time!
CLEOPAS:	Yeah, and we only noticed when He broke the bread!
MARY:	Because we're not too bright!
CLEOPAS:	That's right!
MARY:	But Jesus is alive!
CLEOPAS:	We saw Him for ourselves!
NARRATOR #2:	Suddenly, Jesus appeared in the room with them.
JESUS:	Hey, everyone!
MARY & CLEOPAS:	*(Together, scared)* Ah!
CLEOPAS:	How'd you get in here? The door is locked!
MARY:	Are you a ghost?
JESUS:	*(Sighing)* Here. Feel My hands and side. A ghost doesn't have skin and bones, does it?
MARY:	Um…no.
CLEOPAS:	Not the last time I checked.
MARY:	So it IS You!
NARRATOR #1:	Like I said, they weren't the sharpest knives in the drawer.
JESUS:	Of course, it's Me!... Hey, do you have any food around here? I'm starving.
NARRATOR #1:	So they gave Jesus some broiled fish, and He ate supper with them.

JESUS:	Thanks.
CLEOPAS:	No problem.
NARRATOR #2:	At last, all the promises...
NARRATOR #1:	And the stories of the Bible...
NARRATOR #2:	Finally began to make sense to them.
CLEOPAS:	I get it now.
MARY:	Me too.
JESUS:	It's about time....

NARRATOR #1:	Jesus HAD to die and rise for us to be saved.
NARRATOR #2:	Everything God said was coming true.
NARRATOR #1:	And finally, FINALLY, they believed!
JESUS:	Thank goodness!
EVERYONE:	*(Together)* The end!

(Smile, bow, and then take your seat.)

WHAT IT TAKES TO FOLLOW JESUS

BASED ON:	Matthew 7:13–14, 8:19–22, 16:24–25; Luke 9:57–62, 14:25–35; and John 10:1–21
BIG IDEA:	Following Jesus is a radical commitment that will change your life and the way you live it forever.
BACKGROUND:	Before asking people to become His followers, Jesus made it clear to them that He wasn't willing to take second place in their lives. Following Him is a radical decision that means reprioritizing our relationships, abandoning affections for material things and a comfortable lifestyle, and accepting—even embracing—suffering.
	This script covers some of Christ's teachings about commitment, following Him, and becoming a true disciple of Christ.
KEY VERSE:	*Then Jesus said to his disciples, "Whoever wants to be my disciple must deny themselves and take up their cross and follow me. For whoever wants to save their life will lose it, but whoever loses their life for me will find it"* (Matthew 16:24-25, NIV).
CAST:	You'll need 3-6 children for this skit. If you have a limited number of readers, Narrator #2 can read the parts of all three of the Seekers. In that case, you'll only need three readers for this skit: Narrator #1 (girl or boy), Narrator #2 (girl or boy), Seeker #1 (girl or boy), Seeker #2 (girl or boy), Seeker #3 (girl or boy), Jesus (boy)
PROPS:	None
TOPICS:	Choices, conversion, excuses, following God, priorities, stubbornness
TIPS:	If Narrator #2 is reading the parts of the Seekers, she doesn't turn her back to the audience as the stage directions indicate.
	Position the Narrators on the left side of the stage, Jesus in the center, and the Seekers on the right side of the stage. Bring up the stage lights, and then begin when the listeners are quiet.

What It Takes to Follow Jesus

Director: Lights! Camera! Action!

Narrator #1: Jesus asked His friends...

Narrator #2: To listen to His voice...

Narrator #1: To follow Him...

Narrator #2: And to put Him first.

Jesus: I am the Good Shepherd. My sheep hear Me and listen to My voice. I know them, and they know Me. I have come that they may have life—life to the fullest! I call them by name, and they follow where I go.

Narrator #1: One day, as Jesus was walking along the road with His disciples, a man who had studied the Bible came up to Him.

Seeker #1: Jesus, I'll follow You anywhere!

Jesus: Hmm... Foxes have holes and birds have nests, but I don't have a place to rest. I'm a homeless man. Is that the life you want?

Seeker #1: Hmm... I'll have to think about that.

Jesus: If you want to follow Me, you must love Me more than parents and friends, more than brothers and sisters.

Seeker #1: *(Excitedly)* Love you more than my brothers and sisters? That shouldn't be too tough!

Jesus: You must love Me more than video games and soccer and skateboarding and ice cream and Disney World and cheeseburgers.

Seeker #1: Oh. That's a different plate of potatoes....

Jesus: You must love Me more than life itself. You must carry your cross and follow Me. You must say goodbye to all you own and follow where I go.

Seeker #1: *(Turn your back to the audience.)*

Narrator #1: We never hear of that person again.

Narrator #2: Following Jesus isn't easy.

Narrator #1: It's not always comfortable...

Narrator #2: Or popular...

Narrator #1: And it's not always fun...

Narrator #2: But it's always worth it.

Narrator #1: Then Jesus turned to another person....

Jesus: Follow Me.

Seeker #2: Well, yes.... You see, the thing is...first, let me go and bury my father. Let me take care of some other things first, and then I'll come later.

Jesus: There'll always be things to do. Follow Me now. Let those who are spiritually dead take care of their own.

Seeker #2: Hmm... I'll have to think about that.

Jesus: I've got a special job for you, if you're willing to do it. Tell others about My kingdom. Only those who are spiritually alive can do that.

Seeker #2: I see....

Jesus: So what do you say? Which kind of life do you choose?

Seeker #2: *(Turn your back to the audience.)*

Narrator #2: We never hear of that person again, either.

Narrator #1: Then another person came up to Jesus.

Seeker #3: I'll follow You, Lord, but first, I want to go and say goodbye to everyone at home.

Jesus: *(Sighing)* If you want to begin a journey with Me, you need to be ready to walk all the way with Me. Don't turn around! Don't look back!

Seeker #3: What do you mean?

Jesus: If you're riding a bike and looking back over your shoulder all the time, you're gonna crash. New life with Me lies before you, not behind you in your old way of thinking.

Seeker #3: *(Turn your back to the audience.)*

Narrator #1: Once, Jesus told some stories about what it means to follow Him.

Jesus: You'd never start building a skyscraper without finding out if you're able to pay for it, right?

Narrators: *(Together)* Right!

Jesus: Otherwise, you'd get half done and run out of money, and everyone would laugh at you.

Narrators: *(Together)* Right!

Jesus: Or, if there's a war, you don't go into battle without first figuring out if you have enough soldiers to win, right?

Narrators: *(Together)* Right!

Jesus: Otherwise, you might lose, right?

Narrators: *(Together)* Right!

Jesus: And so it is with Me. Before you say "yes" to Me, you need to decide if you're willing to stick with Me all the way to the end.

Narrators: *(Together)* Right!

Narrator #1: If you won't live for Jesus…

Narrator #2: Don't pretend to be His follower.

Narrator #1: Either Jesus is first in your life…

Narrator #2: Or He's last.

Narrator #1: There's no in-between.

Jesus: Enter through the narrow gate. For wide is the gate and broad is the road that leads to destruction, and many enter through it. But small is the gate and narrow the road that leads to life, and only a few find it (Matthew 7:13–14, NIV).

Narrator #2: Which road will you choose?

Narrator #1: Which path will you walk?

Seeker #1: *(Turn back and face the audience.)* The narrow…

Seeker #2: *(Turn back and face the audience.)* Or the wide?

Seeker #3: *(Turn back and face the audience.)* The one that leads to life…

Narrator #1: Or the one that leads to death?

Narrator #2: The one that leads to Jesus…

Narrator #1: Or the one that goes away from Him?

Jesus: The choice is up to you….

(Silently take your seat.)

A Little Boy Shares His Lunch

BASED ON: Matthew 14:13–21, Mark 6:30–44, Luke 9:10–17, and John 6

BIG IDEA: Jesus miraculously fed more than 5,000 people with a little boy's lunch. He then used this miracle to clarify His true mission and His ability to fulfill our deepest longings.

BACKGROUND: After John the Baptist was killed in prison, his followers buried his body and then reported the news to Jesus. When He heard about it, Jesus left with His disciples to find a quiet place to pray and rest. He needed a chance to mourn the passing of His dear friend and relative.

But the people heard about where He was going, and, by the time His boat reached the beach, there was already a large crowd—5,000 men plus women and children—waiting for them.

Jesus had compassion on them. He taught, healed, and then fed them. Later, He was able to use this miracle as an object lesson to discuss the true nature of His ministry. Yet only after His resurrection did His followers realize the true meaning and importance of His words.

KEY VERSE: *Then Jesus declared, "I am the bread of life. Whoever comes to me will never go hungry, and whoever believes in me will never be thirsty"* (John 6:35, NIV).

CAST: You'll need 8 children for this skit: Narrator #1 (girl or boy), Narrator #2 (girl or boy), Hungry Girl (girl or boy), Hungry Dude (boy or girl), Jesus (boy), Philip (boy), Andrew (boy), Little Boy (boy)

PROPS: None

TOPICS: Compassion, generosity, God's power, Jesus' miracles, priorities, purpose

TIPS: Most of the time the Hungry Girl and the Hungry Dude say their lines together. Whenever they're referred to in the script as the "Crowd," they speak in unison.

Position the Hungry Girl, Hungry Dude, and the Little Boy on the left side of the stage; the Narrators in the center; and Jesus, Philip, and Andrew on the right side of the stage. Bring up the stage lights, and then begin when the listeners are quiet.

A Little Boy Shares His Lunch

DIRECTOR: Lights! Camera! Action!

NARRATOR #1: When Jesus heard that John the Baptist had been killed, He called His friends together.

JESUS: Hey, Andrew!

ANDREW: Yes, Jesus?

JESUS: Gather the rest of the guys and let's go.

ANDREW: Go where?

JESUS: To a quiet place. To rest and pray.

ANDREW: Okay!

NARRATOR #2: They left in the boat so fast that they didn't even have time to grab a bite to eat.

ANDREW: Philip, my tummy is grumbling.

PHILIP: Mine too, Andrew.

ANDREW: Should we say anything to Jesus?

PHILIP: Naw, let's not bother Him about it right now.

ANDREW: Okay!

NARRATOR: People from the area heard where Jesus was going. They followed because they loved to hear Him teach.

CROWD: *(Together)* We like it! We love it!
We want s'more of it!
We like it! We love it!
We want s'more of it!

HUNGRY GIRL: I heard Jesus is on a boat!

HUNGRY DUDE: C'mon! We'll meet Him on the beach!

NARRATOR: So, when the boat landed, there was already a large crowd waiting for Him.

HUNGRY DUDE: There He is! There's Jesus!

HUNGRY GIRL: Hi, Jesus!

JESUS: Hi, there.

PHILIP: Are we still gonna go to a quiet place to pray?

JESUS: No. These people are hurting and hungry for the truth. We'll stay here.

NARRATOR: All day long, Jesus taught the people about God's kingdom and healed those who were sick. Then it started getting dark.

PHILIP: Um, Jesus?

JESUS: Yes, Philip?

PHILIP: It's getting late.

JESUS: I see that.

PHILIP: All these people are getting hungry…

ANDREW: And so are we!

JESUS: Aha.

PHILIP: So…um, maybe we should tell 'em to go and get some food in the nearby towns.

JESUS: Don't send the people away, Philip. You give them something to eat.

PHILIP: Me?

JESUS: Yeah. Fill 'em up, Philip. Take Andrew here and see if you can find them some supper.

PHILIP: Do you want us to order pizzas or something?

JESUS: Um, no.

NARRATOR: So Philip and Andrew went looking for food.

PHILIP: Where are we gonna find enough food for 5,000 men plus their families?

ANDREW: Um, _____? *(Insert the name of a popular local grocery store or restaurant.)*

PHILIP: They don't have any _____s *(the same place as above)* **around here!**

ANDREW: Oh. How about _____? *(another local store or restaurant))*

PHILIP: *(Sighing)* Oh, brother.

NARRATOR: Then Andrew found a little boy.

LITTLE BOY: Goo, goo. Gaa, gaa.

NARRATOR: Um…he wasn't that little.

LITTLE BOY: Oh… Yo, dude!

NARRATOR:	That's better.
ANDREW:	Hey, kid, how much food do you have in your lunch box?
LITTLE BOY:	A couple of fishy sandwiches—five pieces of bread and two little fishies. I had a Twinkie, but I ate it.
PHILIP:	C'mon, let's see if Jesus can use 'em!
ANDREW:	*(Enthusiastically)* Hey! Maybe we can share!
PHILIP:	What?
ANDREW:	Maybe we can share the sandwiches!
PHILIP:	*(Sarcastically)* Yeah, good idea, Andrew. We'll share a couple of fishy sandwiches with 5,000 families!
ANDREW:	Great!
PHILIP:	How are we gonna do that?
ANDREW:	Tell 'em to take itty, bitty bites?
PHILIP:	Oh, brother.
CROWD:	*(Together)* We like it! We love it! We want s'more of it! We like it! We love it! We want s'more of it!
JESUS:	Well, did you find some food?
PHILIP:	Yeah, but this is it—five loaves of bread and two fish.
LITTLE BOY:	Fishies.
PHILIP:	Right.
JESUS:	That'll do.
LITTLE BOY:	I already ate the Twinkie.
JESUS:	No problem.
PHILIP:	How are you gonna feed all these people with just that?
ANDREW:	Have 'em take itty, bitty bites?
JESUS:	I've got a better idea.
NARRATOR:	Jesus had the people sit down in groups of 50. Then He prayed over the food and broke some off and handed it to the disciples.
JESUS:	Here you go. Take what you like and pass the rest around.
NARRATOR:	And the people ate—
CROWD:	*(Together)* We like it! We love it! We want s'more of it! We like it! We love it! We want s'more of it!
NARRATOR:	And ate...and ate...and ate...and ate... until they were full.
PHILIP:	Ah.
ANDREW:	Yummy.
LITTLE BOY:	I wonder if He could do that with Twinkies?
CROWD:	*(Together)* Lots of folks were fed! HUH! Eatin' fish and bread! HUH!
NARRATOR:	Then the disciples went around picking up the leftovers. They found 12 baskets full of food!
ANDREW:	There's more food than we started with!
PHILIP:	You know what that means, don't you?
ANDREW:	Yeah, these people are messy eaters!
PHILIP:	No.
ANDREW:	They took itty, bitty bites?
PHILIP:	Listen! It was a miracle!
ANDREW:	Oh, yeah. That was my next guess.
CROWD:	*(Together)* Lots of folks were fed! HUH! Eatin' fish and bread! HUH!
NARRATOR:	The people were so excited that they wanted to make Jesus the king right then and there!
CROWD:	*(Together)* We like Him! We love Him! We want s'more of Him! We like Him! We love Him! We want s'more of Him!
NARRATOR:	But He quickly sent the disciples away on a boat, and then He slipped away by Himself to pray up on the mountain.
PHILIP:	But, Jesus! How are You gonna get to the other side of the lake without a boat?
JESUS:	You'll see. Now just get going.
NARRATOR:	Later that night, Jesus walked across the water and joined up with His disciples.
PHILIP:	Cool!

ANDREW:	I wish I could do that.
LITTLE BOY:	I wish I had another Twinkie.
NARRATOR:	The next day, the people woke up hungry again. So they went looking for Jesus, hoping for a free breakfast.
CROWD:	*(Together)* Lots of folks were fed! HUH! Eatin' fish and bread! HUH!
JESUS:	You're just here because you want more food!
CROWD:	*(Together)* YUP!
JESUS:	Listen, I didn't come to fill hungry tummies with food. I came to fill hungry souls with God.
CROWD:	*(Together)* Oh.
NARRATOR:	When they heard that, many people stopped following Jesus. Others didn't understand Him.

CROWD:	*(Together)* We're clueless! We're clueless! We haven't got a clue! We're clueless! We're clueless! We haven't got a clue!
NARRATOR:	But some people became even closer to Him.
ANDREW:	We're not gonna leave You, Jesus!
JESUS:	Thank you.
PHILIP:	You're the one who can fill up our souls with God!
JESUS:	You got it!
EVERYONE:	*(Together)* The end!

(Smile, bow, and then take your seat.)

Jesus Heals a Blind Man

Based On: John 9

Big Idea: Jesus healed a man who had been born blind. Then Jesus taught about the importance of His mission to cure inner, spiritual blindness.

Background: The Pharisees refused to believe in Jesus even when the evidence was overwhelming. They rejected Him because they were spiritually blind, but they thought they weren't. Only those who acknowledge their spiritual blindness can ever see spiritual truth and believe in Jesus.

In this story, Jesus once again heals on the Sabbath day, enraging the legalistic Pharisees. In the aftermath of the healing, the man who was born blind gives a compelling testimony to them and becomes a follower of Christ.

We also see a refutation of the popular belief that if something bad happens to someone, God must be punishing him for his sins (John 9:3-5). Jesus explained that sometimes God has something entirely different in mind when He allows bad things to occur.

Key Verse: *He replied, "Whether he is a sinner or not, I don't know. One thing I do know. I was blind but now I see!"* (John 9:25, NIV).

Cast: You'll need 5 children for this skit: Rapper #1 (girl or boy), Rapper #2 (girl or boy), Rapper #3 (girl or boy), Pharisee (boy or girl), Healed Man (boy)

Props: Baseball caps and baggy jackets for the readers (optional)

Topics: Conversion, faith, God's power, healing, Jesus' miracles, new life, Pharisees, questions, second chances, stubbornness

Tips: Since this script is so word-intensive and has a specific rhythm, you'll want to have the readers practice before presenting it to the other students. If you choose to present it as a rap song, give your readers colorful costumes to wear!

To help the readers keep track of the words that are meant to rhyme with each other, and of the overall rhythmic patterns, rhyming words appear in all capital letters. You may wish to demonstrate how to emphasize words that rhyme when reading aloud.

Position the Pharisee on the left side of the stage, the Rappers in the center, and the Healed Man on the right side of the stage. Bring up the stage lights, and then begin when the listeners are quiet.

Jesus Heals a Blind Man

DIRECTOR: Lights! Camera! Action!

RAPPER #1: Yo! Back in the DAY,

RAPPER #2: People used to SAY,

RAPPER #1: If you sinned too much
and you didn't OBEY,

RAPPER #2: God would send a CURSE

RAPPER #1: And make your life WORSE.

RAPPER #2: By making you blind or deaf or LAME!

RAPPER #3: So once there was a man
who'd been blind since BIRTH.

RAPPER #1: He couldn't see the sky,

RAPPER #2: Or the sea,

RAPPER #3: Or the EARTH!

RAPPER #2: And he begged all day
hoping for some MONEY

RAPPER #1: To buy some bread
or butter or HONEY.

EVERYONE: *(Together)* Honey, baby! Honey, baby!
Butter my bread! Honey, baby! Butter
my bread!

RAPPER #3: So the friends of Jesus
came and asked Him WHY,

RAPPER #1: That man was born
so blind in his EYE.

RAPPER #2: "Was it sin in his parents—
in his mom or DAD,
Or sin in himself
that made it so BAD?"

RAPPER #1: "Neither one,"

RAPPER #2: Said Jesus,

RAPPER #1: "Neither he nor THEY.
'Cause God, My Father
doesn't work that WAY!
He's got a bigger purpose,
and He's got a bigger PLAN!"

RAPPER #3: Then Jesus reached out,
and He touched the MAN

RAPPER #2: With some mud

RAPPER #1: That He'd made

RAPPER #3: When He spit in the SAND!

EVERYONE: *(Together)* Spittin', baby! Spittin', baby!
Healin' with mud!
Spittin', baby! Healin' with mud!

RAPPER #1: *(As Jesus)* "Yo!...
Go down to the pool, man,
and wash your EYES.
And when you're done,
you'll get a big SURPRISE!"

RAPPER #2: So he washed that mud;
then he looked AROUND

RAPPER #3: At the sky,

RAPPER #2: And the sea,

RAPPER #3: And the dusty GROUND!

EVERYONE: *(Together)* Whoa, baby! Whoa, baby!
He could see!
Whoa, baby! He could see!

HEALED MAN: I can see the clouds!
I can see the TREES!
I can see the birds
and the buzzin, buzzin' BEES!
I can see the fields
with the green, green GRASSES!
Yo!... I don't even need
a pair of GLASSES!

RAPPER #3: Then all the people
who had seen him BEG

RAPPER #1: Said, "Dude, is it you?
Are you pulling our LEG?"

HEALED MAN: It's me! It's me! I'm him! He's ME!
I used to be blind, but now I SEE!
I can see the clouds!
I can see the TREES!
I can see the birds
and the buzzin, buzzin' BEES!
I can see the fields
with the green, green GRASSES!
Yo!... I don't even need
a pair of GLASSES!

RAPPER #1: "But how?" they said,
and their jaws hung LOW

RAPPER #2: 'Cause they'd never seen anything
like it BEFOW!

HEALED MAN: Well, a man named Jesus
put some mud on my EYES.
And when I washed it off,
I got a big SURPRISE!
I could see the trees and the bees
and the GRASSES!
Yo!... I didn't even need
a pair of GLASSES!

RAPPER #3: "So where's this healer?"

HEALED MAN: Who knows? Not ME.

RAPPER #3: "Then come with us
to the PHARISEES!"

RAPPER #1: But who are they?

EVERYONE: *(Together)* Bible dudes! Bible dudes!
Teaching the law!
Bible dudes! Teaching the law!

RAPPER #1: I tell you...

EVERYONE: *(Together)* Bible dudes! Bible dudes!
Teaching the law!
Bible dudes! Teaching the law!

PHARISEE: If Jesus really helped you,
then it wasn't BLEST
'Cause you're not supposed to heal
on the day of REST!
Tell us how did He do it!
Tell us what did He DO!
Tell us every little thing
that He did to YOU!

HEALED MAN: Like I said before,
He put mud on my EYES.
And when I washed it off,
I got a big SURPRISE!
I could see the trees and the bees
and the GRASSES!
Yo!... I didn't even need
a pair of GLASSES!

PHARISEE: But who do you think
this dude could BE?
'Cause what kind of dude
makes a blind man SEE?

HEALED MAN: It might sound strange,
and it might sound ODD,
But I think He's a prophet
sent down from GOD!

RAPPER #1: Well, the Pharisees doubted.

RAPPER #2: They were full of DOUBT!

RAPPER #1: So they called in his parents

RAPPER #2: To check it OUT!

RAPPER #3: *(As the parents)* "That's him," they said,
"that boy's our SON.
He's always been blind,
and it wasn't much FUN.
But now he can see,
and we don't know HOW,
And all we can say is
'whoa' and 'WOW!'"

RAPPER #1: So one more time
they called him IN.
And they said,

PHARISEE: "It wasn't Jesus
'cause He's full of SIN!"

HEALED MAN: So you say... so you say...
so you say to ME,
But I used to be blind
and now I SEE!
You say He's a sinner,
I don't know if it's TRUE.
But I know this much,
and I say to YOU,
I used to be as blind
as a bat in a TREE,
But now I'm healed.
Yo! Now I SEE!

PHARISEE: But how, how, how
did He help you SEE?

HEALED MAN: I told you before,
but you wouldn't BELIEVE.
Hey, maybe you just
want to hear it AGAIN,
'Cause you wanna believe
and to follow HIM!"

PHARISEE: No way!

RAPPER #1: They screamed,

PHARISEE: That guy's a BUM!
After all, we don't even know
where He's FROM!

EVERYONE: *(Together)* Where's He from? Where's He
from? We don't know! Where's He from?
We don't know!

HEALED MAN: But if Jesus didn't really
come from God on HIGH,
Then He couldn't have healed
my blinded EYE!

EVERYONE: *(Together)* Healer, baby! Healer, baby!
Comin' from God!
Healer, baby! Comin' from God!

Rapper #1: Then the Pharisees all
got really, really MAD,
They'd heard enough.
Yes, sir, they HAD.

Pharisee: You're so full of sin,
God sent you a CURSE!
He made you blind
from the day of your BIRTH!
And the things you believe
are all outta WHACK,
So get outta here now,
and don't ever come BACK!

Rapper #2: When Jesus heard the Pharisees
had kicked him OUT,
He searched till He found him
walkin' ABOUT.

Rapper #1: He said, "Do you believe
in the Son of MAN?"

Healed Man: Tell me who He is,
and I will if I CAN!

Rapper #1: "It's Me! It's Me!
I'm Him! He's ME!
I'm the Light of the World,
and I'll help you SEE.
I've come to heal people,
who are blind INSIDE
And to show proud people
they are really BLIND!"

Rapper #2: And the man smiled big,

Rapper #3: Yeah, he let it SHOW,

Rapper #1: He said, "I believe,"

Rapper #3: And he bowed down LOW.

Rapper #2: And he worshiped the One,
who had helped him SEE.

Rapper #1: 'Cause his eyes had been opened
and his heart set FREE.

Healed Man: Yeah, my eyes had been opened
and my heart set FREE!

Everyone: *(Together)* LIVIN' BABY, LIVIN' BABY,
TOTALLY FREE!
LIVIN' BABY, TOTALLY FREE!
The end!

(Do a rapper pose, bow, and then take your seat.)

THE RETURN OF LAZARUS

BASED ON: John 11:1–45

BIG IDEA: Jesus brought Lazarus back to life in order to bring glory to God and to give the people an opportunity to believe in Jesus.

BACKGROUND: Toward the end of His life, Jesus knew that the Jews were trying to trap Him. Appearing in public was becoming more dangerous than ever for Him. Still, He raised Lazarus from the dead in front of many witnesses, revealing His power and true identity.

Lazarus must have died soon after the messenger left (John 11:3). The messenger's trip of a day to meet up with Jesus, the two-day wait, and then Jesus' day-long trip would account for the 4-day-long span of Lazarus' death.

Contrary to what some people think, Jesus didn't raise His friend from the dead because He was sad or missed him. He did it specifically to bring glory to God and to give people an opportunity to believe. This point is clearly emphasized throughout the story (see John 11:4, 15, 25, 40, 42, 45).

Take note that in many Bibles, a section break appears after verse 44 rather than after verse 45. This is misleading since John 11:45 is the conclusion of the story about Lazarus. (The verse even says "Therefore," indicating that it is the result or culmination of what preceded it.)

In the aftermath of this miracle, the Jews were so committed to extinguishing the excitement about Jesus that they planned to kill both Jesus *and* Lazarus (see John 12:9-10, 17)!

KEY VERSE: *Jesus said to her, "I am the resurrection and the life. The one who believes in me will live, even though they die; and whoever lives by believing in me will never die. Do you believe this?"* (John 11:25-26, NIV).

CAST: You'll need 6-7 children for this skit. If you want, you could have a child wrapped up in toilet paper (or white paper towels) walk into the room and onto the stage when Lazarus appears at the end of the skit. In that case, you would need seven students: Narrator (girl or boy), Messenger (girl or boy), Thomas (boy or girl), Mary (girl), Martha (girl), Jesus (boy), Lazarus (boy, optional)

PROPS: Toilet paper or white paper towels (optional)

TOPICS: Death, faith, friendship, God's power, Jesus' miracles, new life, purpose

TIPS: If you decide to have Lazarus appear at the end of the skit, let it be a surprise. Keep him out of sight until his grand appearance!

Position Mary and Martha on the left side of the stage, the Narrator and the Messenger in the center, and Jesus and Thomas on the right side of the stage. Bring up the stage lights, and then begin when the listeners are quiet.

THE RETURN OF LAZARUS

DIRECTOR: Lights! Camera! Action!

THOMAS: Jesus, there's a messenger here to see you. Mary and Martha sent him.

JESUS: Bring him to Me.

MESSENGER: Sir, Your friend Lazarus is sick. The fever won't leave him. Please come.

THOMAS: Jesus, should I get the others? Do You want to leave?

JESUS: No. We stay here.

THOMAS: But, Master—

JESUS: We stay here. Lazarus' sickness won't end in death. Instead, this has happened to bring glory to God.

NARRATOR: Even though Jesus loved Mary, Martha, and their brother, Lazarus, He stayed there. Then, after two days Jesus called His disciples together.

JESUS: Okay, time to go. Pack up your things. Let's go see Lazarus.

THOMAS: But Jesus, the Jews in that area want to kill You!

JESUS: Yes, I know. But Lazarus has fallen asleep.

THOMAS: Well, that's good then, right? I mean, if he's sleeping then he's gonna get better!

JESUS: Lazarus is dead.

THOMAS: Oh. The Big Sleep.

JESUS: Yeah. He's been dead three days.

THOMAS: Eek. He probably stinks by now.

JESUS: C'mon. Let's go. Trust Me, it's better this way. It'll help you believe.

THOMAS: Alright, everyone, let's go. Let's go and die with Jesus!

NARRATOR: Well, when they arrived, nobody tried to kill them. The people were too sad that Lazarus had died.

MESSENGER: Boo, hoo, hoo... Boo, hoo, hoo...

NARRATOR: When they arrived, Martha hurried out to meet Jesus.

MARTHA: Oh, Master! If only You'd come earlier! You could have saved him! But even now, I know whatever You say will happen.

JESUS: Martha, your brother will live again.

MARTHA: Yes, Lord. One day. When the dead rise at the end of time.

JESUS: I am the Raising of the Dead! I am the Life! If you believe in Me you'll live after you die. And if you live your life believing in Me you'll live forever. Do you believe this?

MARTHA: I do believe! You're the Savior, Jesus! You're God's own Son!

NARRATOR: As they came closer, Mary came out to see Jesus.

MESSENGER: Boo, hoo, hoo... Boo, hoo, hoo...

MARY: Jesus.

JESUS: Mary.

MARY: You could have saved him.

JESUS: Yes.

MARY: But You waited. You waited until he died....

NARRATOR: Many people were there, crying because their friend had died.

MESSENGER: Boo, hoo, hoo... Boo, hoo, hoo...

NARRATOR: It made Jesus very sad.

JESUS: Where is he buried?

MARY: I'll show you.

NARRATOR: When Jesus saw the place where His friend was buried and all the sad people, He cried too.

JESUS: Boo, hoo, hoo... Boo, hoo, hoo...

THOMAS: Look at that! Surely, Jesus loved His friend. Surely, He cared about Lazarus!

MESSENGER: Yeah, right.... If He really cared, why didn't He come sooner? Why didn't He come before it was too late? He heals blind people—surely, He could have healed His friend.

NARRATOR: They led Jesus to the place where they had buried Lazarus. It was a small cave cut out of the rocky hillside. They had covered the entrance with a rock.

MARTHA: Here we are.

MESSENGER: Boo, hoo, hoo... Boo, hoo, hoo...

JESUS: Yes. Now roll the stone away.

MARTHA: But Jesus, he's been dead four days!

JESUS: I know. Roll it away.

MARTHA: His body is all rotting...and he stinketh!

JESUS: Did you say stinketh?

MARTHA: Yeah. It's the King James Version.

JESUS: Oh. Well, anyway, you'll see God's power. I promise.... Now roll the stone away.

NARRATOR: So they did as Jesus said.

JESUS: (Praying) Father God, I know You hear My prayer. But I said this aloud so all these people will know that You hear Me—so that they will believe too.

NARRATOR: And then He turned and looked into the cave.

JESUS: (Loudly) Lazarus! Lazarus! Come out!

NARRATOR: A moment later, the people heard someone inside the cave.

MESSENGER: (Scared) Oh, boy.

NARRATOR: And then, they saw movement.

MESSENGER: (Scared) Yikes.

NARRATOR: Finally, Lazarus stepped out of the cave.

(At this point, if you have a person playing LAZARUS, he can enter, yawn, cross the stage, and hug JESUS.)

MESSENGER: Whoa, mama.

JESUS: Get those grave clothes off him! What does he need with those? He's not dead!

(Skip this next line if you don't use a LAZARUS.)

LAZARUS: Nope. Not anymore! (Flex your muscles.)

NARRATOR: Word spread, and many people believed, just as Jesus had predicted they would.

MESSENGER: He is the Savior! He is the Lord!

NARRATOR: And just like He said, the glory went to God. Lazarus' illness hadn't ended in death—it ended in life!

JESUS: I am the Raising of the Dead! I am the Life! If you believe in Me, you'll live after you die. And if you live your life believing in Me, you'll live forever. Do you believe this?

NARRATOR: And that's the question Jesus asks each of us:

EVERYONE: (Together, pointing at the audience) Do YOU believe this?

(Smile, bow, and then take your seat.)

Peter and the Lame Man at the Beautiful Gate

BASED ON:

Acts 3–4

BIG IDEA:

Peter and John boldly and unashamedly taught people about Jesus. They weren't highly trained theologians, but their message and ministry were inspired and guided by the Holy Spirit.

BACKGROUND:

As the early church grew, Peter and John boldly shared the message of salvation in Christ. One afternoon, on their way to pray at the Temple, Peter healed a man who had been born lame. The miracle caused quite a stir in Jerusalem. As Peter explained that the miracle-working power came from the risen Jesus, the Sadducees bristled with anger and indignation because they didn't believe in the resurrection of the dead.

Since they were influential religious leaders, they had Peter and John thrown into jail for the night. Finally, since they had no reason to keep them and no good way to shut them up, they threatened them and released them.

Peter and John returned to the group of believers and prayed for boldness and clarity in their witnessing. Immediately, God answered their prayer.

KEY VERSE:

Then they called them in again and commanded them not to speak or teach at all in the name of Jesus. But Peter and John replied, "Which is right in God's eyes: to listen to you, or to him? You be the judges! As for us, we cannot help speaking about what we have seen and heard" (Acts 4:18-20, NIV).

CAST:

You'll need 7-10 children for this skit. If you have a limited number of readers, Narrator #2 can read the parts of the Crowd. In that case, you'll only need seven readers for this skit: Narrator #1 (girl or boy), Narrator #2 (girl or boy), Pharisee #1 (boy or girl), Pharisee #2 (boy or girl), 1-3 Crowd (girls or boys), Beggar (preferably a boy), John (boy), Peter (boy)

PROPS:

None

TOPICS:

The Church, conviction, courage, faithfulness, following God, God's power, God's Word, healing, ministry (of the disciples), obedience, Peter, Pharisees, witnessing

TIPS:

If you choose to use more than one person for the Crowd, inform them before the presentation begins that they will say all of their lines together, in unison.

Position the Pharisees on the left side of the stage; the Narrators and the Crowd in the center; and John, Peter, and the Beggar on the right side of the stage. Bring up the stage lights, and then begin when the listeners are quiet.

Peter and the Lame Man at the Beautiful Gate

DIRECTOR: Lights! Camera! Action!

NARRATOR #1: One afternoon, Peter and John were on their way to the Temple.

PETER: Three o'clock!

JOHN: Yup!

PETER: Time to pray!

JOHN: Yup!

NARRATOR #2: As they passed the gate called Beautiful...

PETER: That gate is Beautiful!

JOHN: So they say.

NARRATOR #1: they met a man who couldn't walk. He was over forty years old and had never taken a single step in his whole life.

BEGGAR: That first step's a doozy.

NARRATOR #2: Every day his friends put him by the gate, so he could beg for money.

BEGGAR: Give me gold and silver, please, so I can buy some beets and peas and maybe even mac and cheese! Give me gold and silver, please!

NARRATOR #1: Peter and John stopped next to the begging man.

BEGGAR: Give me gold and silver, please, so I can buy some beets and peas and maybe even mac and cheese! Give me gold and silver, please!

PETER: Sir, look at us.

BEGGAR: *(To yourself)* Oh, goody. They're gonna give me some money!

PETER: I don't have any gold...

BEGGAR: Oh.

PETER: or silver...

BEGGAR: I see.

PETER: but I've got something even better!

BEGGAR: A set of Legos?

PETER: No!

BEGGAR: A kung fu Barbie?

PETER: Listen, I'm gonna heal you! By the power of Jesus, get up and walk!

NARRATOR #2: Then Peter grabbed the man's hand and helped him to his feet.

BEGGAR: Yowsa!

NARRATOR #1: His legs and ankles were healed and strong!

BEGGAR: Whoa, baby!

NARRATOR #2: He was so excited that he started walking...

BEGGAR: *(Walk around.)*

NARRATOR #2: and leaping...

BEGGAR: *(Leap.)*

NARRATOR #2: and praising God!

BEGGAR: I'm walking and leaping and praising God! Hallelujah, sister! Amen, Brother Pete! I'm healed! I'm healed! Praise the Lord!

NARRATOR #1: Right. And everyone who saw him was shocked and amazed.

CROWD: I am shocked and amazed!

PETER: Why are you so surprised? God did this through Jesus! It's His power at work here, not ours!

JOHN: His power, not ours!

PETER: And if you trust in Him, then all of His power...

JOHN: His power, not ours!

PETER: and His forgiveness...

JOHN: His forgiveness, not ours!

PETER: will be yours too!

JOHN: His power, not ours!

NARRATOR #1: Nearby, there was a group of Bible teachers...

NARRATOR #2: Who didn't believe in the raising of the dead.

NARRATOR #1:	They arrested Peter and John because they were teaching the people…
NARRATOR #2:	About the raising of the dead and about Jesus!
NARRATOR #1:	They stuck 'em in jail for the night. But many of the people who'd heard them had believed.
CROWD:	I believe.
NARRATOR #1:	And there were about 5,000 believers.
CROWD:	5,001.
NARRATOR #1:	Right.
NARRATOR #2:	So the next day, the religious council met with all the important leaders to talk to Peter and John.
PHARISEE #1:	So, Peanut Butter and Jelly…
PETER:	That's Peter and John.
PHARISEE #1:	Whatever. Who gave you the power to do this?
PETER:	Jesus.
JOHN:	His power, not ours!
PHARISEE #2:	Who gave you the permission to do this?
PETER:	Jesus.
JOHN:	His permission, not ours!
PETER:	He's the Lord! He's the only one who saves!
JOHN:	His power, not ours!
NARRATOR #1:	The leaders were shocked and amazed by how smart and brave they were.
PHARISEE #1:	I am shocked and amazed!
PHARISEE #2:	Me too.
PHARISEE #1:	Have you two been to college?
PETER & JOHN:	*(Together)* Nope.
PHARISEE #2:	High school?
PETER & JOHN:	*(Together)* Nope.
PHARISEE #1:	Middle school?
PETER & JOHN:	*(Together)* Nope.
PHARISEE #2:	Grade school?

PETER & JOHN:	*(Together)* Nope.
PHARISEE #1:	Preschool?
JOHN:	Something like that.
PHARISEE #2:	Well, how did a couple of preschool dropouts learn so much?
PETER:	Jesus.
JOHN:	His power, not ours!
PHARISEE #1:	Somehow I thought you'd say that….
PHARISEE #2:	Um, go outside while we talk this over.
NARRATOR #1:	So they sent Peter and John out of the room. They didn't want people talking about Jesus, but there was no denying that a great miracle had happened.
NARRATOR #2:	After all, the guy they'd healed…
BEGGAR:	That's me.
NARRATOR #1:	Was still walking…
BEGGAR:	*(Walk around.)*
NARRATOR #1:	and leaping…
BEGGAR:	*(Leap.)*
NARRATOR #1:	and praising God!
BEGGAR:	Hallelujah, sister! Amen and amen!
PHARISEE #1:	What are we gonna do about Peanut Butter and Jelly?
PHARISEE #2:	You mean Peter and John?
PHARISEE #1:	No, I mean peanut butter and jelly. I'm hungry.
PHARISEE #2:	Oh. What about Peter and John?
PHARISEE #1:	Let's threaten to beat 'em up if they don't stop talking about Jesus!
PHARISEE #2:	Good idea.
PHARISEE #1:	Thank you.
NARRATOR #2:	So they called them back in.
PHARISEE #1:	So, Peanut Butter and Jelly…
EVERYONE ELSE:	*(Together, looking at him)* IT'S PETER AND JOHN!
PHARISEE #1:	Whatever. If you don't stop talking about Jesus, you'll be in big trouble!

JOHN:	But Jesus Himself told us to talk about Him! What do you think—should we obey God, or you?
PHARISEE #2:	Is this a trick question?
PETER:	We're not gonna stop.
PHARISEE #1:	Oh, boy.
JOHN:	We're gonna keep telling people about Jesus…
PHARISEE #2:	I was afraid you'd say that.
PETER:	No matter what you do to us!
JOHN:	His power, not ours!
PHARISEE #1:	Err… We'll throw you in jail!
PHARISEE #2:	We'll beat you up!
PHARISEE #1:	We'll take away your Legos!
JOHN:	We don't have any Legos!
PHARISEE #2:	Oh. Then I guess you can go home.
NARRATOR #1:	Right away, when Peter and John were set free, they went back to the other believers and told them the story.
JOHN:	They threatened to take away our Legos.
CROWD:	Ooh…
PETER:	And we don't even have any Legos.
CROWD:	Ooh…
NARRATOR #1:	Then they all prayed…
JOHN:	*(Praying)* God, You're in control.

PETER:	*(Praying)* Help us to be bold and strong.
JOHN:	*(Praying)* Help us to speak Your Word clearly and plainly…
PETER:	*(Praying)* And to keep on doing Your miracles…
JOHN:	*(Praying)* As we keep on serving You.
PETER & JOHN:	*(Together)* Amen!
NARRATOR #1:	Then, when they'd finished their prayer, God's Spirit rocked the house.
CROWD:	Cool.
NARRATOR #1:	He filled their hearts with God's presence…
CROWD:	Radical.
NARRATOR #1:	and their mouths with God's Word.
CROWD:	Awesome.
NARRATOR #1:	God answered their prayer as soon as they'd finished praying it!
NARRATOR #2:	They all spoke His Word boldly and clearly.
NARRATOR #1:	And they got ready…
NARRATOR #2:	For whatever might happen next.
JOHN:	His power, not ours!
EVERYONE:	*(Together)* The end!

(Smile, bow, and then take your seat.)

PHILIP HELPS A MAN FROM ETHIOPIA

BASED ON: Acts 8:26–40

BIG IDEA: Philip, an early missionary to non-Jews, witnessed to the treasurer of Queen Candace of Ethiopia. The man trusted in Christ and became the first Christian convert from the continent of Africa.

BACKGROUND: Philip was one of the men chosen to distribute food to the Grecian Jewish widows (see Acts 6:3-5). Then, after the martyrdom of his coworker, Stephen, he traveled to Samaria and taught there (Acts 8:1-25). Though most Jews hated Samaritans, Philip didn't.

In this story, we hear of Philip responding to the Spirit's urging and finding himself in a position to witness to the treasurer of the country of Ethiopia. The man believed, was baptized, and took the message of Christ back with him to Africa.

In each of these cases, Philip stepped across racial and ethnic lines to witness to people who many Jews would have avoided.

KEY VERSE: *Then Philip began with that very passage of Scripture and told him the good news about Jesus* (Acts 8:35, NIV).

CAST: You'll need 4-6 children for this skit. If you have a limited number of readers, one person could read both the Holy Spirit's and the Angel's parts. In that case, you'd only need five readers for this skit. Narrator #2 could even read both of their parts as well as her own, leaving only four readers. Narrator #1 (girl or boy), Narrator #2 (girl or boy), Angel (girl or boy), Holy Spirit (preferably a boy), Treasurer (preferably a boy), Philip (boy)

PROPS: A cowboy hat and outfit (optional)

TOPICS: Baptism, the Church, conversion, following God, God's Word, grace, Holy Spirit, listening to God, ministry (of the disciples), obedience, repentance, witnessing

TIPS: The Treasurer's character talks and acts like a cowboy for this skit. Let him wear a cowboy hat and outfit for even more fun!

Position the Angel and the Holy Spirit on the left side of the stage, the Narrators in the center, and the Treasurer and Philip on the right side of the stage. Bring up the stage lights, and then begin when the listeners are quiet.

Philip Helps a Man from Ethiopia

Director: Lights! Camera! Action!

Narrator #2: A man named Philip was a leader in the early Christian church.

Narrator #1: He handed out food.

Narrator #2: He was full of wisdom and the Holy Spirit.

Narrator #1: Awesome.

Narrator #2: He could also do miracles!

Narrator #1: Amazing.

Narrator #2: One day he heard an angel of the Lord speak to him.

Angel: Philip, oh, Philip! Oh, listen to me!

Philip: Yeah?

Angel: Go to the desert!
The desert! The desert!
Go to the desert road!

Philip: Did you say the desert?
The desert? The desert?
Did you say the desert road?

Angel: Yes, the desert!
Go to the desert!
Go to the desert road!

Philip: Okay.

Angel: Thank you!

Narrator #1: So Philip went to the desert road.

Angel: Cool.

Narrator #2: And when he got there, God's Spirit spoke to him.

Holy Spirit: Philip, oh, Philip! Oh, listen to Me!

Philip: Yeah?

Holy Spirit: Go to the chariot!
The chariot! The chariot!
Go to the chariot, there!

Philip: Did you say the chariot?
The chariot? The chariot?
The chariot over there?

Holy Spirit: Yes, the chariot!
Go to the chariot!
Go to the chariot, there!

Philip: Okay.

Holy Spirit: Thank you!

Narrator #1: So Philip went to the chariot.

Holy Spirit: Good.

Narrator #1: Then Philip heard another voice...

Narrator #2: But it didn't tell him to go anywhere.

Narrator #1: It didn't even come from God...

Narrator #2: Or an angel.

Narrator #1: It came from a man...

Narrator #2: Who was riding in the chariot.

Treasurer: *(Yelling like a cowboy)* Yeehaw!

Narrator #2: He was in charge of all the treasures of Queen Candace of Ethiopia.

Narrator #1: And the guy was reading aloud from his Bible.

Treasurer: *(Talking like a cowboy)* "He was led like a lamb to the slaughter, and as a sheep before its shearer is silent, so he did not open his mouth.... For he was cut off from the land of the living" (see Isaiah 53:7-8, NIV).

Philip: Hello, there!

Treasurer: Howdy, pardner!

Philip: Do you understand all that stuff you're reading?

Treasurer: Well, how can I unless you teach me? C'mon up here!

Philip: Cool.

Narrator #2: So Philip climbed up into the chariot with the man from Africa.

Narrator #1: And starting with the stuff the guy was reading, Philip explained the Bible to him.

Treasurer: Who's this lamb that Isaiah is writin' about?

PHILIP:	Jesus.
TREASURER:	Aha!
PHILIP:	He was killed, and He didn't complain.
TREASURER:	Whoa, Bessie!
PHILIP:	Life was taken from Him, so He could give new life to us!
TREASURER:	That's what I call a Cool Cowpoke!
PHILIP:	He saved us from our sins!
TREASURER:	*(Yelling like a cowboy)* Yeehaw!
PHILIP:	Do you believe that?
TREASURER:	Why, yes, I do! Jesus is the Savior!
PHILIP:	Cool.
TREASURER:	Hey. Lookee over there! See that lake?
PHILIP:	Yup.
TREASURER:	Well, pardner! What's say I get baptized!
PHILIP:	Let's go!
NARRATOR #2:	So they stopped the chariot and climbed off. They walked into the water, and Philip baptized his new friend.
TREASURER:	*(Yelling like a cowboy)* Yeehaw!
NARRATOR #1:	Then God took Philip to another town to tell more people about Jesus.
HOLY SPIRIT:	It's time to go! To go! To go! It's time to go away!

PHILIP:	Did You say go? It's time to go? It's time to go away?
HOLY SPIRIT:	Yes, it's time. It's time to go! It's time to go away!
PHILIP:	Okay.
HOLY SPIRIT:	Thank you!
NARRATOR #1:	So the Spirit took him away.
PHILIP:	*(Like you're flying through the air)* Aaaaaaah!
HOLY SPIRIT:	Good.
NARRATOR #1:	The man from Africa returned home with a heart full of joy...
TREASURER:	*(Yelling like a cowboy)* Yeehaw!
NARRATOR #2:	And a message full of hope.
TREASURER:	Jesus is the Savior, little doggie!
NARRATOR #1:	And Philip went wherever the Spirit led him, telling more and more people the good news.
EVERYONE:	*(Together)* The end...YEEHAW!

(Smile, bow, and then take your seat.)

SAUL SEES THE LIGHT!

BASED ON: Acts 9:1–22

BIG IDEA: God saved Saul on the road to Damascus. Ironically, he became free—becoming a Christian—on his way to imprison others who were already Christians!

BACKGROUND: After the stoning of Stephen, persecution against the early Christian Church spread rapidly. Saul of Tarsus was an enthusiastic Pharisee dedicated to imprisoning Christians (who at this point in history were called Followers of the Way). On the road to Damascus, Saul had a dramatic conversion experience and became one of the very people he had so violently persecuted.

God had chosen Saul as His messenger to kings, Jews, and most specifically, Gentiles. Saul later changed his name to Paul and wrote a third of the New Testament.

Take note that when Jesus appeared to Saul, He didn't accuse him of attacking His Church, but Himself (see Acts 9:4-6). Why? Because the Church is the body of Christ (see Ephesians 5:23, Colossians 1:24)!

KEY VERSE: *Yet Saul grew more and more powerful and baffled the Jews living in Damascus by proving that Jesus is the Messiah* (Acts 9:22, NIV).

CAST: You'll need 5-6 children for this skit. The Sign Holder doesn't have any lines. All he or she does is hold up the signs at the appropriate times. If you have a limited number of readers, you could have three of the other readers serve as the sign holders: Narrator #1 (girl or boy), Narrator #2 (girl or boy), Sign Holder (girl or boy), Ananias (preferably a boy), Saul (boy), Jesus (boy)

PROPS: Three signs. One that reads, *"Yowsa!"* another that reads, *"Whoa, dude!"* and a third that reads, *"Biiiiiiinnnnggggggg!"*

TOPICS: Anger, calling, the Church, conversion, faith, God's existence, God's Word, listening to God, new life, Paul, repentance, second chances, worship

TIPS: Based on the temperament of your group of students, you may wish to eliminate some of the audience participation sections to shorten this story. If so, cross them out on the scripts of the readers, so they don't inadvertently include them.

Before beginning, explain to the listeners that there are three audience participation parts to this story. Hold up each sign one at a time and practice saying the part aloud with the audience. If you wish, make up gestures to accompany each sign.

Position Ananias and Saul on the left side of the stage, the Narrators in the center, and Jesus and the Sign Holder on the right side of the stage. Bring up the stage lights, and then begin when the listeners are quiet.

Saul Sees the Light!

DIRECTOR: Lights! Camera! Action!

NARRATOR #1: One of the Jewish Pharisees was very smart.

SIGN HOLDER: *(Hold up the "Whoa, dude!" sign, let the audience respond, then set it down.)*

NARRATOR #2: But he didn't like Christians. In fact, he wanted to put them in jail...

SIGN HOLDER: *(Hold up the "Yowsa!" sign, let the audience respond, then set it down.)*

NARRATOR #1: Or even have them killed!

SIGN HOLDER: *(Hold up the "Whoa, dude!" sign, let the audience respond, then set it down.)*

NARRATOR #2: One day he was on his way to arrest some Christians when he saw a bright light.

SIGN HOLDER: *(Hold up the "Biiiiiiinnnngggggg!" sign.)*

NARRATOR #1: He was freaked out.

SIGN HOLDER: *(Hold up the "Whoa, dude!" sign.)*

NARRATOR #2: He fell down with his face to the ground...

SIGN HOLDER: *(Hold up the "Yowsa!" sign.)*

NARRATOR #1: While the light shone on him.

SIGN HOLDER: *(Hold up the "Biiiiiiinnnngggggg!" sign.)*

JESUS: Saul! Saul! Why are you attacking Me?

SAUL: Who are You?

JESUS: I'm Jesus!

SIGN HOLDER: *(Hold up the "Biiiiiiinnnngggggg!" sign.)*

SAUL: Whoa, dude.

SIGN HOLDER: *(Hold up the "Whoa, dude!" sign.)*

JESUS: Now go to the city and I'll tell you what to do.

NARRATOR #2: All the while, the men who were with Saul were freaked out.

SIGN HOLDER: *(Hold up the "Yowsa!" sign.)*

NARRATOR #1: They saw the light...

SIGN HOLDER: *(Hold up the "Biiiiiiinnnngggggg!" sign.)*

NARRATOR #2: But they couldn't understand the voice of Jesus.

NARRATOR #1: Then Saul stood up, but when he opened his eyes, he couldn't see!

SIGN HOLDER: *(Hold up the "Yowsa!" sign.)*

NARRATOR #1: He was blind...

SIGN HOLDER: *(Hold up the "Whoa, dude!" sign.)*

NARRATOR #1: so his friends led him by the hand to the city. For three days he waited and prayed and didn't eat or drink anything.

SIGN HOLDER: *(Hold up the "Yowsa!" sign.)*

NARRATOR #2: In the same city, there lived a believer named Ananias. And God spoke to him in a vision.

SIGN HOLDER: *(Hold up the "Biiiiiiinnnngggggg!" sign.)*

JESUS: Ananias!

ANANIAS: Yes, Lord!

JESUS: Get up and go to Straight Street. There, you'll find Saul. He's praying, and he's blind.

SIGN HOLDER: *(Hold up the "Whoa, dude!" sign.)*

JESUS: He saw you in a vision...

SIGN HOLDER: *(Hold up the "Biiiiiiinnnngggggg!" sign.)*

JESUS: and he knows you're coming to heal him.

NARRATOR #2: But Ananias was afraid!

SIGN HOLDER: *(Hold up the "Yowsa!" sign.)*

ANANIAS: But, Lord, I've heard of this guy! He doesn't like Christians! In fact, he wants to put them in jail...

SIGN HOLDER: *(Hold up the "Yowsa!" sign.)*

ANANIAS: or even have them killed!

SIGN HOLDER: *(Hold up the "Whoa, dude!" sign.)*

JESUS: Go on! I've chosen him to share my story with Jews, with people who aren't Jews, and with kings!

SIGN HOLDER:	*(Hold up the "Whoa, dude!" sign.)*
JESUS:	**And he will suffer much for his faith in Me.**
SIGN HOLDER:	*(Hold up the "Yowsa!" sign.)*
NARRATOR #1:	**So Ananias went. He found Saul and laid his hands on him.**
ANANIAS:	**My brother believer, Jesus sent me! He's the one you saw on the road, in your vision!**
SIGN HOLDER:	*(Hold up the "Biiiiiinnnngggggg!" sign.)*
ANANIAS:	**He wants to heal you and fill you with the Holy Spirit!**
SAUL:	**Whoa, dude.**
SIGN HOLDER:	*(Hold up the "Whoa, dude!" sign.)*
NARRATOR #2:	**So Ananias prayed, and right away, something that looked like scales fell from Saul's eyes…**
SIGN HOLDER:	*(Hold up the "Whoa, dude!" sign.)*
SAUL:	**Yuck!**

NARRATOR #2:	**and he could see!**
SIGN HOLDER:	*(Hold up the "Biiiiiinnnngggggg!" sign.)*
NARRATOR #1:	**Saul got up and got baptized.**
SAUL:	**Cool.**
NARRATOR #2:	**He ate and drank at last. Then he told other people that Jesus really is the Savior.**
SAUL:	**Jesus really is the Savior!**
SIGN HOLDER:	*(Hold up the "Whoa, dude!" sign.)*
NARRATOR #1:	**He wanted others to believe in Jesus too!**
SIGN HOLDER:	*(Hold up the "Biiiiiinnnngggggg!" sign.)*
SIGN HOLDER:	*(Hold up the "Yowsa!" sign.)*
SIGN HOLDER:	*(Hold up the "Whoa, dude!" sign.)*
EVERYONE:	*(Together)* **The end!**

(Smile, bow, and then take your seat.)

PAUL, BARNABAS, AND THE ONE TRUE GOD

BASED ON:	Acts 14:8–20
BIG IDEA:	Paul survived being stoned and immediately returned to preach to the people who had tried to kill him.
BACKGROUND:	As Paul traveled around preaching about Jesus, he found fierce resistance among the Pharisees and Jewish religious leaders—the very people who had, at one time been his coworkers.
	In this story, he is stoned and presumed dead after miraculously healing a man who had been born lame. Paul survived the stoning and immediately returned to the city. Paul didn't let a little thing like attempted murder get in his way of sharing the Good News!
KEY VERSE:	*They stoned Paul and dragged him outside the city, thinking he was dead. But after the disciples had gathered around him, he got up and went back into the city* (Acts 14:19-20, NIV).
CAST:	You'll need 8-10 children for this skit: Narrator #1 (girl or boy), Narrator #2 (girl or boy), Person #1 (girl or boy), Person #2 (girl or boy), 1-3 Pharisees (boys or girls), Barnabas (preferably a boy), Paul (boy), Lame Man (boy)
PROPS:	None
TOPICS:	Conviction, courage, faithfulness, following God, God's existence, healing, ministry (of the disciples), obedience, Paul, perseverance, Pharisees, witnessing
TIPS:	Sometimes Person #1 and Person #2 say their lines together. Whenever they are referred to in the script as the "Crowd," they speak in unison. Note that the Lame Man only has a couple of lines. You may want to point this out to the person reading those lines so he doesn't feel left out.
	This story contains a number of uncommon names. Be sure that your students know how to pronounce "Lystra," "Hermes," "Zeus," and "Barnabas."
	Position the Crowd and the Lame Man on the left side of the stage, the Narrators and the Pharisees in the center, and Paul and Barnabas on the right side of the stage. Bring up the stage lights, and then begin when the listeners are quiet.

Paul, Barnabas, and the One True God

DIRECTOR: Lights! Camera! Action!

NARRATOR #1: Paul and Barnabas went to the town of Lystra…

NARRATOR #2: Because the Jews in the other towns wanted to kill them.

PHARISEES: *(Together, singing to the tune of "Here We Come A-Caroling")*

Here we come arre-esting,
arre-esting you all!
Here we come to mur-urder
a lou-oudmouth named Paul!
Love and joy come to you
when our mission is all through!
And God bless you,
we'll kill you all today! Yes, today!
And God bless you,
we'll kill you all today!

NARRATOR #2: Now, the people in Lystra worshiped lots of made-up gods.

NARRATOR #1: One was named Zeus.

NARRATOR #2: He was their main god.

NARRATOR #1: And one was named Hermes.

NARRATOR #2: He was the messenger of the gods.

NARRATOR #1: As Paul and Barnabas came near to the city, they noticed a temple.

BARNABAS: C'mon, Paul, the city is just up ahead!

PAUL: Look, Barnabas! A temple to Zeus!

BARNABAS: Whoa. They're getting ready to sacrifice those bulls to their gods!

PAUL: These people really need to hear about Jesus!

BARNABAS: C'mon, let's go tell 'em!

NARRATOR #2: When they entered the city, Barnabas let Paul do most of the talking.

BARNABAS: I'm a man of few words.

NARRATOR #1: And as Paul was teaching the people about Jesus and telling them the good news…

NARRATOR #2: He noticed a man who couldn't walk.

LAME MAN: My feet don't work.

NARRATOR #2: The man was listening carefully to Paul.

LAME MAN: I feel defeated.

NARRATOR #1: He was sad that he'd never been able to walk.

LAME MAN: I feel the agony of defeat.

NARRATOR #2: But when Paul saw that the man had faith in God…

NARRATOR #1: Enough faith to get healed…

NARRATOR #2: Paul said…

PAUL: Stand up! Get on your feet right now and walk!

NARRATOR #2: And he did!

LAME MAN: Whoa…I have overcome defeat!

NARRATOR #1: When the crowds saw that, they were amazed.

PERSON #1: I'm amazed!

PERSON #2: Me too.

PERSON #1: They must be gods!

PERSON #2: It's Zeus and Hermes!

PERSON #1: They've come down for a visit!

PERSON #2: Let's worship them!

BARNABAS: Um, Paul…

PAUL: Yeah, Barnabas?

BARNABAS: This isn't good.

PAUL: No, it isn't. They're bringing the bulls over here!

BARNABAS: They're gonna worship US!

NARRATOR #2: When Paul and Barnabas saw what was going on, they were very upset.

NARRATOR #1: All the people started shouting…

CROWD: *(Together)* The gods have come down! The gods have come down!

PAUL: No, no! You've got it all wrong!

CROWD:	*(Together)* The gods have come down! The gods have come down!
BARNABAS:	We're people like you! We're not gods!
PAUL:	We've just come here to tell you about the one TRUE God!
CROWD:	*(Together)* The gods have come down! The gods have come down!
BARNABAS:	Alright, already!... Listen up for a minute!
CROWD:	*(Together)* Listen up! The gods are talking! Listen up to what they say!
PAUL:	Oh, brother.... We're not gods!
BARNABAS:	The one true God made everything!
PAUL:	He gives you rain!
CROWD:	*(Together)* Ooh!... We like the rain!
PAUL:	Good! And He gives you seasons.
CROWD:	*(Together)* Ooh!... We like the seasons!
BARNABAS:	Good! And He lets your crops grow!
CROWD:	*(Together)* Ooh!... We like the crops!
PAUL:	Good! He gives you all this stuff to prove that He's there. He feeds you and takes care of you to show you that He's real.
PERSON #1:	That was a nice speech!
PAUL:	Thank you.
PERSON #2:	Now it's our turn!
BARNABAS:	Oh, no.
CROWD:	*(Together, loudly)* THE GODS HAVE COME DOWN! THE GODS HAVE COME DOWN!
PAUL:	Somehow I thought you'd say that.
NARRATOR #1:	The people still wanted to worship them, but finally Paul and Barnabas stopped them.
BARNABAS:	Thank goodness.
PAUL:	No kidding.
NARRATOR #2:	Then something strange happened.
NARRATOR #1:	You mean the first part of this story ISN'T strange?

CROWD:	*(Together)* The gods have come down! The gods have come down!
NARRATOR #2:	The Jews who hated Paul came to town.
BARNABAS:	Oh, no. Not again.
NARRATOR #1:	They told the crowds that Paul and Barnabas were bad people...
PHARISEES:	*(Together)* They're bad people.
NARRATOR #1:	with a dumb message...
PHARISEES:	*(Together)* With a dumb message.
NARRATOR #2:	And that they should kill them.
PHARISEES:	*(Together, singing to the tune of "Here We Come A-Caroling")* Here we come arre-esting, arre-esting you all! Here we come to mur-urder a lou-oudmouth named Paul! Love and joy come to you when our mission is all through! And God bless you, we'll kill you all today! Yes, today! And God bless you, we'll kill you all today!
NARRATOR #1:	And the crowds believed them!
PERSON #1:	They're not gods!
PERSON #2:	They're imposters!
CROWD:	*(Together)* Kill the imposters! Kill the imposters!
BARNABAS & PAUL:	*(Together)* Uh-oh.
NARRATOR #1:	They picked up stones and threw them at Paul until they thought he was dead.
PERSON #2:	That should do it!
PAUL:	Ouch.
NARRATOR #2:	Then they dragged him outside the city.
PAUL:	Ouch.
BARNABAS:	Whoa.
NARRATOR #1:	So the crowds went from wanting to worship them to wanting to kill them!
NARRATOR #2:	Yup. Just like the crowds did with Jesus.
NARRATOR #1:	Aha.
NARRATOR #2:	But then a strange thing happened.

NARRATOR #1: Oh, no. Not again.

NARRATOR #2: Paul DIDN'T die that day. The believers gathered around him to help him up.

PAUL: I'm not dead.

BARNABAS: That's good!

PAUL: I'm alive.

BARNABAS: That's good!

PAUL: Let's go back to the city!

BARNABAS: That's crazy!... They just tried to kill you! And now you wanna go back and preach to them?

PAUL: Yup!

NARRATOR #2: So Paul jumped up and went back to the city.

BARNABAS: *(Sighing)* Okay, Paul...here I come.

NARRATOR #1: And the next day he and Barnabas left the city, but soon they returned.

NARRATOR #2: Paul knew the message of Jesus was so important that he was willing to share it with people...

NARRATOR #1: Even if they tried to kill him because of it.

EVERYONE: *(Together)* The end!

(Smile, bow, and then take your seat.)

101

PAUL IS SHIPWRECKED!

BASED ON: Acts 27–28

BIG IDEA: On the way to Rome, the ship on which Paul and Luke were sailing was caught in hurricane-force winds. After the shipwreck, many sailors and islanders heard about and witnessed God's power and grace.

BACKGROUND: Paul had been imprisoned. As a Roman citizen, he had the right to appeal his case to Caesar. When he did that, a Roman soldier named Julius was put in charge of assuring that he arrived safely in Rome.

Immediately after starting their trip, they ran into bad weather. The story of their shipwreck and the survival of all 276 sailors and passengers is a testament to God's grace and provision.

KEY VERSE: *Last night an angel of the God to whom I belong and whom I serve stood beside me and said, "Do not be afraid, Paul. You must stand trial before Caesar; and God has graciously given you the lives of all who sail with you" (Acts 27:23-24).*

CAST: You'll need 6 children for this skit: Sailor #1 (boy or girl), Sailor #2 (boy or girl), Julius (preferably a boy), Aristarchus (preferably a boy), Luke (boy), Paul (boy)

PROPS: None

TOPICS: Conviction, fear, God's sovereignty, God's Word, ministry (of the disciples), Paul, witnessing

TIPS: Luke and Aristarchus serve as the narrators of this story. (Even though all the characters in this story are male, feel free to use some girls as readers.)

Position Luke and Aristarchus on the left side of the stage, the Sailors in the center, and Paul and Julius on the right side of the stage. Bring up the stage lights, and then begin when the listeners are quiet.

PAUL IS SHIPWRECKED!

DIRECTOR: Lights! Camera! Action!

LUKE: Hi, I'm Dr. Luke. I wrote the book of Acts and the book of Luke.

ARISTARCHUS: And I'm Aristarchus. I didn't write anything, but I'm good friends with Paul. I travel with him and help him.

LUKE: And do we have a story for you today!

ARISTARCHUS: We were all on a boat, on a trip to Rome.

LUKE: We set sail for Italy, but the winds weren't with us.

ARISTARCHUS: We finally managed to get to a place called Fair Havens.

LUKE: Winter was coming, and we couldn't sail during the winter months. So we had to decide—should we stay or should we go?

ARISTARCHUS: The captain wanted to leave.

SAILOR #2: I wanna leave!

LUKE: So Paul talked to the crew.

PAUL: Men, this trip is gonna end in disaster!

SAILOR #1: Bummer.

PAUL: Ships, cargo, and even people are gonna be lost!

SAILOR #1: Major bummer.

PAUL: We should wait until spring before we sail!

SAILOR #1: Oh, goody! A winter vacation!

LUKE: But the soldier leading the voyage disagreed.

JULIUS: Oh, c'mon! We'll be alright. The ship's captain says so!

SAILOR #2: I says so!

SAILOR #1: Oh.

SAILOR #2: Heave ho!

JULIUS: Let's go!

SAILOR #1: Oh, no.

LUKE: And so...we left.

ARISTARCHUS: But before long, a storm blew in.

SAILOR #1: Bummer.

ARISTARCHUS: It was as strong as a hurricane!

SAILOR #2: Oopsy.

PAUL: Told you so.

LUKE: We couldn't fight the wind, so we just let it drive us along.

SAILOR #1: Major bummer.

SAILOR #2: Major oopsy.

LUKE: We had to tie ropes around the boat just to hold it together!

ARISTARCHUS: And we had to lower the anchors so we wouldn't crash on the sandbars!

LUKE: The storm was so bad that we started throwing cargo overboard, just as Paul had predicted we would.

SAILORS: *(Singing together, to the tune of "Row, Row, Row Your Boat")*

Throw, throw, throw your stuff
deeply in the sea!
Toss the cargo overboard;
I'm glad it isn't me!

ARISTARCHUS: By the third day, we were cutting up sails and tossing them into the ocean too!

SAILORS: *(Together, singing)* Toss the sails overboard;
I'm glad it isn't me!

LUKE: The storm went on for many days. The whole time we never saw the sun or the stars.

ARISTARCHUS: Finally, we gave up all hope of being saved.

SAILOR #1: Think we'll make it?

SAILOR #2: Not a chance.

ARISTARCHUS: No one wanted to do anything or even eat!

SAILOR #1:	I don't wanna do anything.
SAILOR #2:	I don't wanna eat.
LUKE:	Then Paul spoke to the sailors again.
PAUL:	Men, it's like I said before. We should never have sailed in the first place!
SAILOR #1:	No kidding.
SAILOR #2:	Thanks for reminding me.
PAUL:	But now have courage! No one will lose his life.
SAILORS:	*(Together)* Yeah, right.
PAUL:	Last night God's angel told me the ship will be destroyed!
SAILORS:	*(Together)* Bummer.
PAUL:	But we'll all be saved!
SAILORS:	*(Together)* Oh. Cool.
LUKE:	So for two weeks we drifted along, until one night we heard shouting on the deck.
SAILOR #2:	I think we're getting close to land!
SAILOR #1:	Me too!
SAILOR #2:	Measure the water.
SAILOR #1:	120 feet deep!
SAILOR #2:	That's good. Measure it again!
SAILOR #1:	Now it's only 90 feet deep!
SAILOR #2:	That's bad! We're gonna crash!
SAILOR #1:	Now it's only 4 inches deep!
SAILOR #2:	What?
SAILOR #1:	Just kidding!
SAILOR #2:	Drop the anchors! Don't let her run ashore!
SAILOR #1:	*(Whispering)* Hey, we gotta get outta here. Let's pretend to lower an anchor and sneak away!
SAILOR #2:	Good idea.
PAUL:	We'll never survive if those men leave. Stop 'em!
JULIUS:	Cut the ropes! Let the lifeboat loose!
LUKE:	And the lifeboat just floated away….
SAILOR #1:	*(Sadly)* Bye-bye, Mr. Lifeboat!
SAILOR #2:	*(Sadly)* Bye-bye, Mr. Last Chance of Sneaking Away and Saving Ourselves Before We Crash.
ARISTARCHUS:	Now everyone HAD to trust what Paul said.
SAILOR #1:	No kidding.
SAILOR #2:	Thanks for reminding me.
PAUL:	Men, it's been two weeks, and you haven't been eating. Go on! Eat something and get your strength back. Trust me.
SAILOR #1:	I want a hot dog.
SAILOR #2:	I'll take a peanut butter, pickle, and broccoli sandwich.
LUKE:	Then, in front of everyone, Paul thanked God for the bread, and all 276 people on board ate.
SAILOR #1:	That's a lot of bread.
SAILOR #2:	That's a lot of peanut butter and pickles!
SAILOR #1:	And broccoli.
SAILOR #2:	Right!
ARISTARCHUS:	After supper, we tossed the extra wheat overboard into the sea to lighten the load.
SAILORS:	*(Singing together, to the tune of "Row, Row, Row Your Boat")* Throw, throw, throw your wheat deeply in the sea! It's getting really soggy there; I'm glad it isn't me!
LUKE:	In the morning, we saw a beach up ahead, and we ran the ship aground.
SAILOR #1:	We crashed on land.
SAILOR #2:	We crash-landed!
ARISTARCHUS:	The front of the ship was stuck, and the back of the ship was getting smashed apart by the roaring waves.
SAILORS:	*(Screaming)* Roar!
PAUL:	Oh, brother.

LUKE:	That's when some of the soldiers decided to kill the prisoners, so they couldn't escape.
SAILOR #2:	I'll kill Paul!
SAILOR #1:	I'll kill everyone else!
JULIUS:	No! I want to save Paul. Don't hurt any of them!
SAILOR #1:	But...
JULIUS:	I'm in charge here. I say don't hurt anyone!
SAILOR #1:	Oh, no! The boat is busting up!
SAILOR #2:	Quick, everyone, swim for shore!
SAILOR #1:	What if I don't know how to swim?
SAILOR #2:	Wear floaties!
SAILOR #1:	What?
SAILOR #2:	Or grab a plank and float on that! Hurry! Before the ship breaks apart!
LUKE:	So that's what we did. And when we were all safely ashore, we found out that the island was called Malta.
ARISTARCHUS:	The people there were very kind and friendly.
SAILOR #1:	You want a Malta?
SAILOR #2:	No, but I'll have a milkshake!
LUKE:	They made a big bonfire, and we all gathered around it to warm up.
SAILORS:	*(Together, smiling)* Cool...I mean, warm!

ARISTARCHUS:	Suddenly, a deadly snake slithered out of the firewood and bit Paul!
SAILORS:	*(Together)* Bummer.
LUKE:	But he didn't fall over dead!
SAILORS:	*(Together)* Cool.
ARISTARCHUS:	So the people of the island thought he was a god.
SAILORS:	*(Together)* Funky.
LUKE:	But of course, we explained who the REAL God is.
SAILORS:	*(Together)* Cool.
ARISTARCHUS:	Then Paul healed the governor's father and other people too.
LUKE:	We stayed there about three months, until spring.
SAILORS:	*(Together)* Vacation!... Vacation!... A winter vacation!
LUKE:	God was in control. And all those sailors...
ARISTARCHUS:	And the people on the island...
LUKE:	saw the power of God and heard His mighty Word.
SAILORS:	*(Together)* God rocks!
ARISTARCHUS:	No kidding!
EVERYONE:	*(Together)* The end!

(Smile, bow, and then take your seat.)

Scripture Verse Index

Old Testament Verses

Genesis 2: "Adam, Eve, and a Sneaky Snake"

Genesis 2:15: "Adam, Eve, and a Sneaky Snake"

Genesis 3: "Adam, Eve, and a Sneaky Snake"

Genesis 6—9: "Noah and the Zoo Cruise"

Genesis 18:1-15: "A Son for Sarah and Abraham"

Genesis 21:1-7: "A Son for Sarah and Abraham"

Genesis 22:1-19: "God Tests Abraham's Faith"

Genesis 37—50: "Joseph's Journey from the Pit to the Palace"

Numbers 24:17: "The Arrival of the Wise Men"

Joshua 6:12-21: "God Makes Walls Fall at Jericho"

Ruth 1—4: "Naomi's New Family"

1 Samuel 2:27-36: "Samuel and the Voice in the Night"

1 Samuel 3: "Samuel and the Voice in the Night"

1 Samuel 17:1-52: "David and the Giant Problem"

1 Kings 3: "Solomon's Radical Wisdom"

1 Kings 4:29-34: "Solomon's Radical Wisdom"

1 Kings 17:1: "Elijah and the Showdown on Mt. Carmel"

1 Kings 18:1-46: "Elijah and the Showdown on Mt. Carmel"

2 Chronicles 1:1-13: "Solomon's Radical Wisdom"

Esther 1—8: "Esther, the Bravest Beauty Queen"

Isaiah 53:7-8: "Philip Helps a Man from Ethiopia"

Daniel 3: "Funny Names and a Fiery Furnace"

Daniel 6: "Daniel in the Lions' Den"

Jonah 1—4: "Jonah and the Basking Shark"

New Testament Verses

Matthew 1:18-25: "The Birth of King Jesus"

Matthew 2:1-12: "The Arrival of the Wise Men"

Matthew 5:16: "Daniel in the Lions' Den"

Matthew 7:13-14: "What It Takes to Follow Jesus"

Matthew 8:19-22: "What It Takes to Follow Jesus"

Matthew 12:38-42: "Jonah and the Basking Shark"

Matthew 14:13-21: "A Little Boy Shares His Lunch"

Matthew 16:24-25: "What It Takes to Follow Jesus"

Matthew 20:1-16: "Jonah and the Basking Shark"

Matthew 21:1-11: "The First Palm Sunday"

Matthew 27:11-54: "The Death of Jesus"

Matthew 27:55—28:10: "Jesus Is Alive!"

Mark 6:30-44: "A Little Boy Shares His Lunch"

Mark 11:1-11: "The First Palm Sunday"

Mark 15:1-5: "The Death of Jesus"

Mark 15:40—16:11: "Jesus Is Alive!"

Luke 1:26-38: "The Birth of King Jesus"

Luke 2:1-7: "The Birth of King Jesus"

Luke 9:10-17: "A Little Boy Shares His Lunch"

Luke 9:57-62: "What It Takes to Follow Jesus"

Luke 14:25-35: "What It Takes to Follow Jesus"

Luke 15:11-32: "Jonah and the Basking Shark"

Luke 19:28-44: "The First Palm Sunday"

Luke 23:1-25: "The Death of Jesus"

Luke 24:1-12: "Jesus Is Alive!"

Luke 24:13-43: "The Road to Emmaus"

John 6: "A Little Boy Shares His Lunch"

John 9: "Jesus Heals a Blind Man"

John 10:1-21: "What It Takes to Follow Jesus"

John 11:1-45: "The Return of Lazarus"

John 12:9-10, 17: "The Return of Lazarus"

John 12:12-19: "The First Palm Sunday"

John 18:28-40: "The Death of Jesus"

John 18:36: "The First Palm Sunday"

John 19:25: "The Road to Emmaus"

John 20:1-18: "Jesus Is Alive!"

Acts 4:20: "Samuel and the Voice in the Night"

Acts 6:3-5: "Philip Helps a Man from Ethiopia"

Acts 8:26-40: "Philip Helps a Man from Ethiopia"

Acts 9:1-22: "Saul Sees the Light!"

Acts 10:34-35: "Naomi's New Family"

Acts 14:8-20: "Paul, Barnabas, and the One True God!"

Acts 27—28: "Paul Is Shipwrecked"

Romans 4:16-17: "God Tests Abraham's Faith"

Romans 5: "Adam, Eve, and a Sneaky Snake"

Romans 8:28: "Joseph's Journey from the Pit to the Palace"

Romans 8:31: "David and the Giant Problem"

Romans 13:8: "Adam, Eve, and a Sneaky Snake"

Romans 15:7: "Adam, Eve, and a Sneaky Snake"

2 Corinthians 1:20: "A Son for Sarah and Abraham"

2 Corinthians 3:12: "Elijah and the Showdown on Mt. Carmel"

Galatians 3:6-9: "A Son for Sarah and Abraham"

Galatians 3:13: "Adam, Eve, and a Sneaky Snake"

Galatians 4:4-5: "The Birth of King Jesus"

Galatians 4:5: "Naomi's New Family"

Galatians 5:13: "Adam, Eve, and a Sneaky Snake"

Ephesians 4:32: "Adam, Eve, and a Sneaky Snake"

Ephesians 5:23: "Saul Sees the Light!"

Ephesians 6:12: "God Makes Walls Fall at Jericho"

Philippians 1:20: "Esther, the Bravest Beauty Queen"

Colossians 1:24: "Saul Sees the Light!"

Titus 2:14: "Naomi's New Family"

Hebrews 3:13: "Adam, Eve, and a Sneaky Snake"

Hebrews 11:7: "Noah and the Zoo Cruise"

Hebrews 11:8-19: "God Tests Abraham's Faith"

James 1:5: "Solomon's Radical Wisdom"

1 Peter 1:22: "Adam, Eve, and a Sneaky Snake"

1 Peter 3:15: "Funny Names and a Fiery Furnace"

1 Peter 3:18: "The Death of Jesus"

1 Peter 3:18-21: "Noah and the Zoo Cruise"

1 John 4:11: "Adam, Eve, and a Sneaky Snake"